Timesavers for Teachers, Book 2

Report Card and IEP Comments, Substitute Teacher Instructions Kit, and Classroom Awards and Passes, with CD

Stevan Krajnjan

JOSSEY-BASS
A Wiley Imprint
www.josseybass.com

Published by Jossey-Bass
A Wiley Imprint
989 Market Street, San Francisco, CA 94103-1741—www.josseybass.com

Readers should be aware that Internet Web sites offered as citations and/or sources for further information may have changed or disappeared between the time this was written and when it is read.

Limit of Liability/Disclaimer of Warranty: While the publisher and author have used their best efforts in preparing this book, they make no representations or warranties with respect to the accuracy or completeness of the contents of this book and specifically disclaim any implied warranties of merchantability or fitness for a particular purpose. No warranty may be created or extended by sales representatives or written sales materials. The advice and strategies contained herein may not be suitable for your situation. You should consult with a professional where appropriate. Neither the publisher nor author shall be liable for any loss of profit or any other commercial damages, including but not limited to special, incidental, consequential, or other damages.

Jossey-Bass books and products are available through most bookstores. To contact Jossey-Bass directly call our Customer Care Department within the U.S. at 800-956-7739, outside the U.S. at 317-572-3986, or fax 317-572-4002.

Jossey-Bass also publishes its books in a variety of electronic formats. Some content that appears in print may not be available in electronic books.

ISBN: 978-0-4703-9533-2

Library of Congress catalog information available from publisher

Printed in the United States of America

FIRST EDITION

PB Printing   10 9 8 7 6 5 4 3 2 1

Table of Contents

Part II: Substitute Teacher Instructions Kit

Part III: Classroom Awards and Passes

To my family Ana, Laura, Leah, and Lucas Krajnjan

About This Book

This book is a comprehensive collection of ready-to-use report card and IEP comments, a substitute teacher instruction kit, and interactive classroom awards that are designed to help teachers simplify work, personal organization, record keeping, and classroom management. The interactive CD included makes it possible for you to type information directly on the forms, save and/or print the file, modify information, and access it with ease.

Part I, Report Card and IEP Comments, includes over 1,800 report card and Individual Education Plan (IEP) comments organized in a ready-to-use format. Just select the comment that most accurately matches the level of achievement, insert the student's name into the comment, and cut and paste it into the report card template. Key words are in bold type and the comments are ranked by topic and nature and ordered from most positive to most negative, making sight reading and search easy for busy teachers.

All comments have been labeled for your convenience and ease of search with the following abbreviations:

G (General comment)—indicates different levels of achievement

G,N (General/Negative)

P,P (Very Positive)

P (Positive)

P,N (Positive/Negative)

N (Negative)

N,N (Very Negative)

N,N,N (Very, Very Negative)

NS (Next Steps)

This is by no means an exhaustive list of comments, but a helpful collection of ideas, sentences, and phrases designed to make your report card–writing process a lot less frustrating and time consuming. Comments can be easily modified to suit your personal assessment needs.

Part II of the book includes an entire Substitute Teacher Instructions Kit. Having to be away from the classroom often results in teachers leaving hastily written instructions and last-minute lesson plans. There never seems to be enough time to leave the kind of individual instructions you would like or to inform the substitute teacher about specialized classroom routines. This section allows the classroom teacher to develop detailed substitute teacher instructions only once and to use these instructions over and over again! The only updating to be done will be that of the daily lesson plans. This organized and highly efficient method will allow both the classroom teacher and the substitute teacher to devote valuable time to other important matters in the classroom.

Part III includes the most commonly used classroom awards, certificates, and school passes, all ready to print and use. Several versions of some forms are included.

All students deserve recognition for their good attitude, hard work, academic excellence, and outstanding performance. Use these awards often to help motivate students and let them know their efforts are appreciated.

Free yourself from the time-consuming burden of having to create your own classroom forms from scratch. Be a well-organized and better prepared teacher by using this book, and have more time for other things in life!

And if you find these forms helpful, you might also like *Timesavers for Teachers, Book 1: Interactive Classroom forms and Essential Tools with CD*, also from Jossey-Bass Teacher, available at local bookstores and online retailers.

About the Author

Over his extensive teaching career, Stevan Krajnjan has learned that teaching is a complex job, and time a very precious commodity for every educator. It became obvious to him early on that busy teachers are always looking for ways to lessen the ever-increasing demand on their professional and personal time. This observation led Stevan to develop his popular, often-used materials that help teachers become well-organized, better prepared, and—most importantly—leave them with more time. These materials were first introduced on his Web site, timesaversforteachers.com, and are now available in this and other Timesavers for Teachers books.

Stevan attended McMaster University where he played varsity tennis and graduated with a Bachelor of Arts degree. He received his Bachelor of Education degree from the University of Toronto and acquired Specialist qualifications in Computers in the Classroom and Special Education. A full-time teacher since 1985, Stevan teaches Special Education in Brampton, Ontario, Canada, where he resides with his wife, Ana, and their three children, Laura, Lucas, and Leah. In 1997 Stevan was presented with an Exceptional Teacher Award by The Learning Disabilities Association of Mississauga and North Peel in recognition for outstanding work with children with learning disabilities.

In addition to teaching and designing timesaving teacher resources, Stevan enjoys dabbling in art and competing in provincial tennis tournaments. Stevan was a provincially ranked tennis player throughout the last 30 years. In recognition of his sports accomplishments, Stevan was recently inducted into the *City of Brampton Sports Hall of Fame*.

For more information on Stevan and his timesavers, see www.timesaversforteachers.com.

Part I

Report Card and IEP Comments

Introductory Comments

- _____ has made (*some/ good/ excellent*) **progress** this term. **(G)**

- _____ **remains focused** in class, but (*often/ occasionally/ rarely*) **needs reminders** to **stay on task**. **(G)**

- _____ **consistently takes responsibility for** his/her **own share of the work** when participating in class and group activities. He/she **remains focused** in class, but (*often/ occasionally/ rarely*) **needs reminders** to **stay on task**. **(G)**

Positive

- _____ is a **leader** in his/her class who cooperates **with others** and always **tries to work above** and **beyond** the **assigned tasks**. **(P,P)**

- _____ is a **highly motivated** student who **participates** in class activities with **creativity** and a great deal of **enthusiasm**. His/her **willingness to lead**, **organize,** and **inspire** others is **well noted**. **(P,P)**

- _____ 's **work often exhibits thought** and **care**. **(P)**

- _____ **works well independently** and **with others**. **(P)**

- _____ **consistently participates** in class and **group** activities. **(P)**

- _____ is a **cooperative student** who **works well** with **other classmates**. **(P)**

- _____ shows effective **time-management** and **organizational skills**. **(P)**

- _____ shows **self-direction** in **goal setting** and **goal achievement**. **(P)**

- _____ shows (continues to demonstrate) a **keen interest in learning**. **(P)**

- _____ has put forth a **consistent effort in all areas** of his/her work this term. **(P)**

- _____ consistently builds forms **positive relationships** with peers and adults. **(P)**

- _____ has been a **very helpful, courteous, polite,** and **hardworking** student. **(P)**

- _____ 's **enthusiasm for learning is reflected in** his/her **effort to do things well**. **(P)**

- _____ shows **good leadership skills** when working with classmates in **groups**. **(P)**

- _____ has made a **good adjustment** to his/her new school in a short period of time. **(P)**

- _____ **continues** to **work well independently** and **shows good motivation** in class. **(P)**

- _____ is a **very considerate** student who **enjoys learning** and **works well with others**. **(P)**

- _____ is a **cooperative**, **pleasant**, and **quiet** student who is **genuinely motivated to learn**. **(P)**

- _____ **has experienced successful integration** in several academic subjects this term. **(P)**

- _____ is an **enthusiastic** learner who **enjoys group activities** and **socializing** with his/her peers. **(P)**

- _____'s **diligent work habits** and **exemplary behavior** have contributed to this term's **good achievement**. **(P)**

- _____ **works well cooperatively** and **independently** to achieve his/her academic goals. **(P)**

- _____ has **maintained excellent progress** this term. **Self-motivation** to learn has been **quite evident**. **(P)**

- _____ **actively participates** in class and **demonstrates leadership** in a wide range of learning activities. **(P)**

- _____ **usually follows** classroom **routines** and **instructions independently**, and **puts forth** a **good effort**. **(P)**

- _____ **shows self-direction** in learning and **usually completes homework on time** and **with care**. **(P)**

- _____ **follows** classroom and school **routines**, **shares materials** and equipment, and **plays cooperatively** with others. **(P)**

- _____ possesses **strong leadership potential** and is encouraged to provide leadership in a variety of groupings. **(P)**

- _____ **demonstrates** a **genuine concern** for **learning** and approaches given tasks with a **sincere desire to succeed**. **(P)**

- A **conscientious individual**, _____ has **set goals** for **personal achievement** and is **working diligently** to attain them. **(P)**

- _____'s **positive** and **consistent efforts** toward school and learning activities have resulted in a **very successful year**. **(P)**

- _____ continues to be a **cooperative** and **constructive member** in group activities who is **well liked** by his/her peers. **(P)**

Report Card and IEP Comments

- _____ **approaches new learning opportunities** with **confidence** and demonstrates a **positive attitude** toward learning. **(P)**

- _____ **always completes** his/her **work independently**. _____ **welcomes new tasks** and **seeks new opportunities** for learning. **(P)**

- _____ continues to be a **conscientious, cheerful student** who **assumes volunteer positions** to **aid** his/her **peers** and **teachers**. **(P)**

- _____ is an **exemplary student** whose **considerate manners** and **happy, friendly demeanor** have earned him/her many **friends** among peers. **(P)**

- _____ recognizes where and how **assignments** would benefit from additional information. He/she **integrates learning from various subject areas**. **(P)**

- _____ is a **motivated, happy** learner who **enjoys being with** his/her **peers** and **working on group projects**. _____ **participates well** in class. **(P)**

- _____ **continues to strive to do** his/her **best** in all areas of learning. He/she **works well** with **limited supervision** and **uses** his/her **time effectively**. **(P)**

- _____ is a **conscientious student** who **always completes tasks accurately** and **with care**. He/she **works well independently** and **in a group setting**. **(P)**

- _____ is a **quiet, independent student** who **uses class time well**. His/her **classmates value** him/her **as a thoughtful, productive member** of any (the) group. **(P)**

- _____ **consistently listens** and **respects** the **opinions** of others. _____ **communicates effectively** and **contributes information** to the class and **group** members. **(P)**

- _____ willingly **works with others**. He/she **shows respect** for **ideas of others** in our class. **(P)**

- _____ **follows** routines and **instructions independently**. He/she **sometimes solves problems** independently. **(P)**

- _____ **participates enthusiastically** in class activities and **follows classroom** and school **procedures** consistently. **(P)**

- _____ **communicates well** with class and group members. He/she **often interprets** and **understands problems**. **(P)**

- _____ **shows motivation** and **self-confidence**. He/she **consistently uses** his/her **time effectively** and **remains on task**. **(P)**

- _____ **shows motivation** and self-confidence. He/she **puts forth** a **consistent effort** and **seeks positive solutions to conflict**. **(P)**

- _____ usually **works willingly** and **collaboratively** with **others**. He/she **contributes information** and **ideas** to the class. **(P)**

Report Card and IEP Comments

5

- _____ **effectively interprets** and **synthesizes information** and **always participates** in class **with eagerness** and **enthusiasm**. (**P**)

- _____ often **participates** in class and **group** activities. _____ **asks questions** to **clarify meaning** and **ensure understanding**. (**P**)

- _____'s **reading** and **writing** skills are **improving** slowly. _____ is showing **increased willingness to focus** and **complete** assigned **work** in class. (**P**)

- _____ **accepts various roles** within the class and group, including **leadership**. He/she asks **questions** to clarify meaning and **works willingly with others**. (**P**)

- _____ **continues to show improvement** on most of his/her programs. He/she **shares** his/her **ideas** and **research skills** in preparing for **group presentations**. (**P**)

- _____ **shows motivation, initiative,** and **self-direction**. _____ is **encouraged** to **analyze** and **assess accurately** the **value** and the **meaning of information**. (**P**)

- _____ is a very **conscientious** student who **forms positive relationships** with peers and adults. He/she **works well in groups** and **always follows classroom** and **school procedures**. (**P**)

- _____ has **adjusted well** to his/her new surroundings and the _____ program. _____ is **well accepted** by his/her peers and **works well** with others in **small groups**. (**P**)

- _____ **accepts responsibility for completing tasks on time** and **with care**. _____ **works well without supervision**. _____ shows a **positive attitude** toward learning. (**P**)

- _____ is a **cooperative, polite class member** who **volunteers to help others**. He/she **regularly displays a positive attitude** toward learning and **follows classroom** and **school procedures**. (**P**)

- _____ **consistently takes responsibility for** his/her **own share of the work** when participating in class and **group activities**. He/she **remains focused** and (rarely) needs reminders to stay on task. (**P**)

- _____ **shows motivation** and **self-confidence**. _____ **puts forth** a **consistent effort** and seeks **positive solutions** to **conflict**. He/she is encouraged to participate in **class discussions**. (**P**)

- _____ is a **considerate** and **energetic** student who has **adjusted** (fairly) **well** to the routines and expectations of the classroom. His/her **willingness to lead** and **organize** class activities is **noted** and **appreciated**. (**P**)

- _____ **always accepts responsibility** for **completing tasks on time** and **with care**. _____ **follows classroom routines** and **instructions independently** and displays a **positive attitude** toward learning. (**P**)

- _____ 's **work** often **exhibits thought** and **care**. He/she **works well cooperatively** and **independently** to achieve his/her academic goals. _____ is **encouraged** to **seek assistance prior to test** dates. (**P**)

- _____ **welcomes new tasks** and **seeks new opportunities** for **learning**, especially when it involves **group work**. He/she has **demonstrated a positive attitude toward learning** and shown (good/ excellent/ great) **leadership skills**. (**P**)

- _____ **has successfully taken advantage of all the learning opportunities** that our program had to offer this year. He/she has **worked hard throughout the year** and (greatly/ impressively) **contributed to the positive** class atmosphere. (**P**)

- _____ is a **quiet, polite** member of the class. _____ **routinely** and **independently works well** in a **group setting**. _____ **displays a positive attitude toward** learning, **demonstrating motivation** and seeking new learning opportunities. (**P**)

- _____ **continues to make positive gains** in the _____ program, namely in the area of **organizational skills**. _____ **now listens to teacher advice** and suggestions and **is making** an **effort to become** a **better organized student**. (**P**)

- _____ **consistently completes** and **submits** all **assignments** for evaluation **on time**. _____ **works well independently**, shows **good motivation,** and is a **risk taker**, especially when working on tasks that require **problem solving** and **creativity**. (**P**)

- _____ consistently **seeks work** and **new opportunities** for learning. He/she **contributes positively** to class **discussions** and cooperative group activities. _____ is encouraged to **assess** his/her **own work** and identify **goals** to strive for. (**P**)

- _____ is a **highly motivated independent learner** who is to **be commended** for his/her **high level** of **achievement** this term. _____ is a **role model** for other students in terms of **ability** to **focus** on the **task** and **consistent completion of work** with high quality. (**P**)

- _____ (consistently/ always) **completes assignments** on time. He/she **begins work promptly** and **accepts responsibility for** his/her **own learning**. _____ is encouraged to **participate in group** and class **discussions** and to accept a variety of roles within the class, including **leadership**. (**P**)

- _____ **continues to improve** his/her **confidence** in presenting ideas and concerns in **group** and class **discussions**. His/her level of **focus** and **concentration** have **improved**. He/she is **developing greater self-control** in all work situations, and has **established realistic goals** for himself/herself for the next term. (**P**)

- Although a **quiet individual,** _____ **enjoys sharing** his/her **ideas** and concerns with his/her classmates in **small group** discussions. Throughout the (*next/ following/ second/ third*) term, _____ is encouraged to continue to build on his/her achievements and work on **communication skills** and level of **self-confidence**. (**P**)

- _____ **has established some personal challenges** for his/her programs, especially in the area of **reading expectations**. A more **conscientious** individual, _____ **has**

Report Card and IEP Comments

set goals for his/her own achievement and is **working diligently** to attain them. He/she is **encouraged to maintain** this **positive, responsible attitude** throughout the (*next/ final*) term. (**P**)

- This term _____ has made **some gains** in his/her program. He/she continues to maintain a **high level of commitment** and (*enthusiasm/ exuberance*) toward learning. _____ demonstrates a **good ability to work independently** and in **groups**. _____ is **encouraged to express** his/her **opinions more often** during class discussions in order to develop his/her **leadership** abilities. (**P**)

- _____ **approaches new challenges** and tasks **with motivation, eagerness,** and **confidence**. _____ is able to use **information** and different **technologies effectively** and has, consequently, **experienced** a **good deal of success** this term. He/she **willingly accepts various roles** within the class and **group** situations, including the role of a **leader**. (**P**)

- _____ is **developing** suitable **research skills** necessary in the preparation for **oral, group presentations**. He/she **enjoys sharing** his/her **ideas** and concerns in small group discussions. _____ is encouraged to concentrate on achieving his/her **personal goals** for the (*next/ final*) term, including a **more risk-taking** approach **to new** and challenging **learning situations**. (**P**)

- _____ **continues to show improvement** in many areas of the program this term. He/she **shares** his/her **ideas** and **research skills** in preparing for **group presentations**. _____ has established some personal challenges for his/her programs, especially in the area of **reading expectations**. A **conscientious individual**, _____ has **set goals** for **personal achievement** and is **working diligently** to attain them. (**P**)

- _____ has experienced **good progress** in **many areas** of the program. He/she has **improved** his/her level of **commitment** and **concentration** on **daily tasks** and long-term **group** and **individual assignments**. He/she **has displayed** a **more cooperative approach** to both his/her **work** and his/her **classmates**. _____ is **to be congratulated** on his/ her **achievements** and encouraged to continue in this more **positive, responsible** manner throughout the final term. (**P**)

- _____ has encountered **good success** in many of the programs this term. He/she **uses** his/her organizer to record important information and due dates. He/she **shares** his/her **ideas** and concerns **in group** and class **discussions**, and is a **cooperative, responsible** individual. _____ is becoming a more **confident risk-taker** with his/her assignments. **Careful planning** and a **conscientious attitude** are **positive** aspects of his/her **class participation and behavior**. He/she is encouraged to maintain solid **effort** throughout the next term. (**P**)

Positive/Negative

- _____ is a **considerate student** who **has had some difficulty adjusting to the** (*academic/ learning*) **expectations** of the classroom. (**P,N**)

- _____ often **contributes information** and **ideas** to the class or group. He/she **sometimes follows routines** and **instructions** independently. (**P,N**)

- _____ regularly participates in class and group activities. _____ is encouraged to approach all subjects and problems with a positive attitude. (P,N)

- _____ is an energetic student who participates in class activities with enthusiasm and works well with others, but often needs reminders to stay focused. (P,N)

- _____ is a friendly person who gets along well with his/her peers. _____ approaches new tasks reluctantly and often needs teacher prompts, encouragement, and reminders to begin and complete school work. (P,N)

- _____ is a quiet individual who usually follows classroom routines and school procedures. _____ is encouraged to express his/her opinion in class more often and come to class prepared with adequate school equipment. (P,N)

- _____ is a considerate and very polite student who has adjusted well to the _____ program and his/her new school setting. _____ continues to need regular assistance with many aspects of the academic program. (P,N)

- _____ is (generally) a very considerate student who continues to have some difficulty completing assignments on time. Establishing a consistent study and homework routine must become one of _____'s second-term goals. (P,N)

- _____ is a considerate and energetic student who has adjusted (fairly) well to the routines and expectations of the classroom. He/she is often able to work cooperatively in small groups, yet has had some difficulty working independently. He/she is encouraged to seek remedial assistance. (P,N)

- _____ is an active participant in group learning activities. He/she consistently demonstrates respect and consideration for adults and peers. _____ (sometimes) needs reminders and encouragement to begin tasks and remain focused in class. (P,N)

- _____ shows self-direction in learning and usually completes homework on time and with care. _____ usually investigates and obtains information independently. _____ is encouraged to participate in class discussions and group activities. (P,N)

- _____ has expressed an eagerness to do better in the area of academics, but has some difficulty reaching some of the outlined goals. He/she continues to require (some/ frequent) reminders to use his/her class time to complete assignment tasks or seek clarification. (P,N)

- _____ is a considerate student who has had some difficulty adjusting to the academic expectations of the classroom. He/she is often able to work cooperatively in small groups, yet has had some difficulty working independently to achieve academic success. (P,N)

- _____ has made some gains in his/her academic program this term. He/she more readily expresses his/her opinions in class, and often seeks clarification about assignments. He/she is reminded to put forth initiative toward all written work in order to experience further success. (P,N)

- _____ **cooperates well** with his/her classmates and teachers, but (*at times/ often*) **needs reminders** to remain **on task, not speak to others**, and **wander** around during class time. _____ is **eager to do well** in class but **often needs teacher support** to help **organize** and use **written information**. **(P,N)**

- _____ **works well independently** and is **consistently on task**. He/she **demonstrates self-direction** in learning. _____ is encouraged to participate more frequently in class and **group discussions**. **(P,N)**

- _____ **shows interest** and **curiosity** and **helps others** in the classroom. _____ is encouraged to **participate** in class **discussions** and **group** activities. He/she is also **encouraged** to put forth a more consistent **effort. (P,N)**

- _____ identifies and **pursues learning tasks independently** and **with great deal of enthusiasm**. _____ **contributes ideas** and **information** to the class, but **often needs reminders to complete written tasks** to the best of his/her ability. **(P,N)**

- _____ is a very **curious** and **cheerful** individual who always **contributes ideas** and **information** to the class. _____ **welcomes new tasks** and **seeks new opportunities for learning, but** at times **needs encouragement to work to the best of** his/her **ability. (P,N)**

- _____ is a very **curious** individual who (*often/ always*) **contributes ideas** and **information** to the class. _____ **welcomes new tasks** and **approaches new learning opportunities with confidence. Greater focus** in class **would help** improve quality of academic work. **(P,N)**

- _____ is usually **focused, but occasionally needs reminders to stay on task.** He/she usually **organizes information** logically and manages it **effectively.** _____ is encouraged to **participate** in class and **group** activities and to **ask questions** to **clarify meaning** and **ensure understanding. (P,N)**

- _____ is making **gradual gains** this year **in handling challenges** at school. His/her **daily attendance** has **improved** (greatly). **Many accommodations** have been put in place for him/her to experience success at school. _____ is encouraged to continue to accept small **challenges** and develop his/her **self-concept. (P,N)**

- _____ continues to seek teacher clarification for assignments, but is **encouraged to include detail** and all the **criteria** in his/her **final work.** _____ shows a **good ability to work in groups** and **independently.** _____ is encouraged to express his/her opinions more often during class discussions in order to develop his/her **leadership** abilities. **(P,N)**

- _____ has expressed an **eagerness to do better** in his/her academics, **yet** has had **difficulty reaching some of** the goals. _____ **continues to require frequent reminders to use** his/her **class time to complete assigned tasks** or to seek (*explanation/ clarification*). _____ is **reminded to work toward** his/her **personal best** and **refrain from excessive socializing. (P,N)**

- _____ has made **some gains** in his/her **academics.** _____ continues to **work well independently**, but has had **some difficulty working in small groups** this term. _____ has a **great deal of potential** that would facilitate him/her becoming an academic leader in our class. He/she is encouraged to put forth greater effort in order to accomplish goals set for himself/herself. (P,N)

- _____ is a conscientious and responsible student who has adjusted well to the routines and expectations of the classroom. _____'s work often exhibits thought and care. He/she works well cooperatively and independently to achieve his/her academic goals. _____ is encouraged to develop confidence in his/her ability to communicate ideas in class discussions. (P,N)

- This term, _____ continues to develop himself/herself as an academic leader. He/she maintains enthusiasm and effective organizational skills toward his/her academics and cocurricular activities. _____ continues to work well independently, but has had some difficulty working in groups. He/she is encouraged to stay focused and keep the socializing to a minimum. (P,N)

- _____ has expressed an eagerness to do better in his/her academics this term, yet has had difficulty reaching some of his/her goals. He/she continues to require regular reminders to use his/her class time to complete assignment tasks and seek clarification. He/she needs to demonstrate consideration for his/her classmates by refraining from (frequent/ regular) outbursts and focus on his/her academics. (P,N)

- This term, _____ has made some gains in his/her program. _____ continues to seek (explanation/ clarification) for assignments, but is encouraged to include detail and all the criteria in his/her written work and school organizer. _____ demonstrates a good ability to work in groups and independently. He/she is encouraged to express his/her opinions more often during class discussions. (P,N)

- This term, _____ has made some academic gains in our program. He/she continues to seek (explanation/ clarification) for assignments and demonstrates diligence toward his/her projects. _____ is encouraged to incorporate greater detail in all his/her written work in order to maximize success. He/she is encouraged to express personal opinions more often during class discussions to further, promote, and practice leadership abilities. (P,N)

- This term, _____ continues to make academic gains in our program. He/she continues to seek (explanation/ clarification) for assignments and shows diligence toward his/her projects. _____ works well independently and is beginning to feel more comfortable working in unfamiliar group settings. _____ is encouraged to express personal opinions more often during class discussions in order to develop leadership abilities. (P,N)

- _____ is a cooperative student who willingly participates in class activities. _____ requires reminders to remain on task, not speak to others, or wander around the classroom during lessons. He/she is encouraged to seek advice and teacher assistance as an alternative to getting out of seat and striking up unrelated conversations. _____ is eager to do well, but continues to need teacher support to help organize and use written information. (P,N)

- _____ has had difficulty reaching some of his/her goals this term. He/she continues to require frequent reminders to use his/her class time to complete assignment tasks or seek (explanation/ clarification). _____ is encouraged to use his/her school **organizer** more effectively by scheduling weekly remedial sessions. _____ continues to **work well independently**, but has had **some difficulty working in groups**. _____ is **encouraged to stay** focused and **refrain from excess socializing**. (**P,N**)

- _____ has **demonstrated good ability to** work in groups **under close teacher supervision**. _____ often continues to **speak out of impulse**, with a **limited sense of when to stop interrupting others**. (**P,N,N**)

- _____ is a **cheerful** student who **enjoys verbal participation** and continues to make regular, **important contributions** to class **discussions**. _____ often **speaks out of impulse**, with a **limited sense of when to speak** and **for how long. Frequent distractibility** and **lack of focus** (*are/ remain*) a concern. (**P,N,N**)

- **Remaining on task** for extended periods of time **is difficult** for _____; however, a **positive change in attitude**, and a **desire to improve are evident.** (**N,P**)

- _____ has **made a number of positive gains** in **many areas** of **learning skills** this term. He/she is **learning to work independently, without interrupting** his/her peers, and **more homework assignments** have been **completed** than in the past. **Remaining on task** for extended periods of time **is difficult** for him/her; however, a **positive change in attitude** and a **desire to improve are evident.** (**N,P**)

Negative

- _____ **needs frequent reminders** to stay **focused** and refrain from **interrupting.** (**N**)

- _____ is **encouraged to show motivation** and **contribute to cooperative problem** solving. (**N**)

- _____ is **encouraged to develop confidence** in his/her ability to **communicate ideas** in class **discussions.** (**N**)

- _____ is **encouraged to work on organizational skills** and **use class time more effectively** (productively). (**N**)

- _____ is **encouraged to seek assistance** prior to **test** dates in order **to ensure** that **concepts** are **understood.** (**N**)

- _____ has made **limited progress** in **areas of organizational skills, homework completion, social skills,** and **interpersonal relationships.** (**N**)

- **Greater consistency in homework completion,** improved **study habits,** and **regular participation** in **class would help** improve academic achievement. (**N**)

- _____ has had **difficulty reaching some** of his/her **goals.** He/she **continues to require frequent reminders to use** his/her **class time** for **completion** of **assignment tasks** or **seek** (*further explanation/ clarification*). (**N**)

- This term, _____ has **put forth more effort** toward his/her academic program; however, he/she has had **difficulty keeping to due dates** for submitting **homework** for evaluation. _____ **is aware** of the need for him/her to seek **remedial assistance** on a regular basis. **(N)**

- _____ has put forth **some effort** toward his/her program; **however**, he/she has had **some difficulty keeping to due dates** for homework evaluations. He/she continues to **require some reminders** to **use** his/her **class time** for **completion** of **assigned tasks** or **seeking clarification**. He/she is **encouraged to be considerate** of his/her classmates by **refraining from** (frequent) **outbursts** and **focus instead on academic progress**. **(N)**

- _____ **has experienced some difficulty** in **adjusting** to the **expectations** of his/her programs. He/she **uses** his/her **organizer** to **record important events, dates,** and **information**. However, he/she **needs to improve** his/her **level of commitment** and **concentration on daily tasks** and **long-term assignments**. He/she **is attempting to display a more cooperative approach to** his/her **work** and his/her **classmates**. To be successful, _____ is **encouraged to** combine a positive, **responsible attitude** with **diligent effort**. **(N)**

- _____ has been **absent from school** on quite a few occasions this term. _____ is **able to work cooperatively** and **independently** to achieve his/her academic goals **when fully committed** to a task. **Despite ample class time** and **remedial opportunities**, some **homework** and long-term **assignments remain unfinished**. Timely **completion of homework** and regular, daily use of the school organizer **must be in place** if _____ is to continue to experience success in academic subjects. **(N)**

- _____ is an **enthusiastic participant** in a wide range of learning (classroom) activities but **needs to learn to work on following teacher instructions**. **(N,N)**

- **In spite of** (frequent/ repeated) **reminders, requests,** and **parent communication,** _____'s **lack of cooperation** continues to **undermine** the **classroom learning environment**. **(N,N)**

- _____ is **an active participant** in a wide range of learning (classroom) activities but **needs to learn to work** on **listening** to **ideas** of **others without interrupting. In spite of frequent reminders, requests,** and **parent communication, lack of cooperation continues** to **undermine** the **classroom learning environment**. **(N,N)**

Completion of Writing Tasks

Positive

- _____ **demonstrates responsibility** in attendance, punctuality, and **task completion**. (**P**)

- **Some progress was observed**, and _____ is **to be commended** for his/her **enthusiasm** and **desire to succeed**. (**P**)

Positive/Negative

- _____ **continues to strive to write to the best of** his/her **ability. To help** him/her **with completion** of this task, he/she has been provided with **access to computers spell checkers**, and taught the **prewriting** and **proofreading strategies. Writing** is an area that **requires continued attention** for _____. He/she **must** carefully **proofread** and **edit** all work that is to be submitted for marking. (**P,N**)

Negative

- **Positive reinforcement** and **adult encouragement have enabled** _____ **to complete writing tasks** this term. _____ is very **reluctant to produce written work** and has been offered a variety of options with which to express his/her ideas. (**N**)

- _____ **needs constant encouragement to begin** and **complete writing activities**. It would be advantageous for _____ to use his/her **cursive writing** when copying notes. _____ should continue to practice creating **jot notes to help** him/her **stay on task**. (**N**)

- _____ was not able to demonstrate an understanding of the materials covered in class, as he/she **did not begin** or **complete** (*any/ most*) **class assignments**.

- _____ **did not seek additional assistance although this option was offered** to him/her on a daily basis. (**N**)

- **Inconsistent homework completion remains a** (serious) **concern** and a hindrance to learning. _____ **does not** always **put forward** a **consistent effort** in **writing**. _____ is very **reluctant to produce detailed written work** and has been offered a variety of options with which to express his/her ideas. **Positive reinforcement** and **adult encouragement have enabled** _____ **to complete writing tasks** this term. (**N**)

Report Card and IEP Comments

Writing/Printing

General

- Assessment indicates that _____. **(G)**

- Personal writing (*rarely/ sometimes/ often/ consistently*) shows good **reasoning** and **understanding and ability to communicate ideas**. **(G)**

- _____ (*with teacher assistance/ with some assistance/ often/ successfully*) **completes** written **assignments**. **(G)**

- _____ writes (*few/ one or more/ numerous*) **simple sentences** that contain **appropriate punctuation**. **(G)**

- _____ (*with teacher assistance/ with some assistance/ often/ successfully*) **completes** written assignments **in paragraph form**. **(G)**

- _____ (*with teacher assistance/ with some assistance/ often/ successfully and clearly*) writes using an **introduction**, **body**, and a **conclusion**. **(G)**

- _____ (*rarely/ sometimes/ often/ consistently*) **shows ability to spell** effectively and use correct **punctuation** and **grammar** conventions. **(G)**

- Important **supporting details** in _____'s writing are (*generally unclear/ recognizable/ reasonably clear/ very clear/ make sense*). **(G)**

- _____ (*with teacher assistance/ with some assistance/ often/ successfully and clearly*) **uses writing as a way** of **communicating** ideas (to others). **(G)**

- _____ (*with teacher assistance/ with some assistance/ often/ successfully and clearly*) uses writing that **contains an introduction**, **body**, and a **conclusion**. **(G)**

- **Transitions** are (*not used/ rarely used/ generally used where needed/ used appropriately and skillfully to connect ideas throughout the tex*t). **(G)**

- **Main idea** and **reason for writing** in _____'s work are (*very unclear/ generally unclear/ recognizable/ reasonably clear/ very clear*). **(G)**

- _____ writes in **paragraph form** (*only with teacher assistance/ with little teacher assistance/ independently/ independently and without error*). **(G)**

- _____ (*with teacher assistance and encouragement/ with some assistance and encouragement/independently/ routinely/ effectively*) **uses** the **proofreading checklist** sheet. **(G)**

- **Revision** of (own) written work **is done** (*with teacher assistance/ with some teacher assistance/ routinely and successfully, without a reminder*). **(G)**

- _____ (*rarely/ sometimes/ often/ consistently*) shows **effective spelling, punctuation,** and **grammar rules** in (*personal/ own*) writing. (*Extensive/ Moderate/ Minimal/ No*) **revision** is required. **(G)**

- _____ (*with teacher assistance/ occasionally/ usually*) **conveys ideas and information** for various/different **purposes** and to **defined audiences**, using **forms of writing** appropriate for the identified purpose and topic. (**G**)

- _____ (*rarely/ sometimes/ often/ consistently*) **shows *(depth of thought, correct sequencing, ability to stay on topic), communicate clearly*** for a purpose, and create an **effective plan** for writing. (**G**)

- _____ (*with teacher assistance and encouragement/ with some assistance and encouragement/independently/ routinely/ effectively*) uses the **"thought web"** (graphic organizer) **sheet to produce** better/well **organized written work**. (**G**)

- _____(with teacher assistance/sometimes/ usually/consistently/ independently) **describes the main idea** in informational materilas (nonfiction and novel reading responses), and **explains how** the outlined **details support the main ideas. (G)**

- _____ (*with assistance/ sometimes/ usually/ consistently/ independently*) is able to tell the **main idea** in written materials, and **expound how the written details** support the main ideas, based on _____ and _____ reading responses. (**G**)

- _____ (has dificulty being able/ often has difficulty being able/ sometimes is able) to **organize information** to develop a **central idea**, using **well-connected** and **well-written paragraphs**. This was evident in _____ (**G**)

- **Introduction** and **conclusion** (*are not clear, or are often omitted/ sometimes show effective components/ are often fairly strong and effective, showing good connection to the main idea/ are very strong and effective and relate to the main idea*). (**G**)

Positive

- **More than one paragraph** is **used** in writing. (**P**)

- **Shows consistency** in the **cursive writing form**. (**P**)

- _____ **is making an effort** to write **independently**. (**P**)

- Written work is **better organized, clear, logically sequenced**. (**P**)

- **Improvement** in writing **technique/handwriting is noticeable**. (**P**)

- _____ is **able to write a passage several sentences long**. (**P**)

- _____ **has become aware of** the **need** to write **in paragraph** form. (**P**)

- _____ **experiences a higher degree of success** in **organizing ideas**. (**P**)

- _____ shows evidence of **effort to improve** the **quality** of written work. (**P**)

- Is **able to produce meaningful writing** for assigned **tasks** and **audiences**. (**P**)

- **Written ideas** are **well linked** through the use of **linking words** and **paragraphs**. **(P)**

- **Conferences with peers** and **teacher** in order to **produce** a **good-quality, published written work**. **(P)**

- _____ is **to be commended for** the **frequent use** of **sophisticated words** in his/her written work. **(P)**

- _____ **pays attention to** whether or not his/her writing needs an **introduction** and a **conclusion**. **(P)**

- _____ **continually strives to improve**, and is **always a willing participant in** our **writing activities**. **(P)**

- _____ **uses better organized** and **linked paragraphs**, and **is working hard to improve** in this area. **(P)**

- **Journal reflections** (*were/are*) **well thought out** and **many opinions** and o**bservations** (*were/are*) recorded. **(P)**

- **Positive reinforcement** and adult **encouragement have enabled** _____ **to complete writing tasks** this term. **(P)**

- _____ 's work reveals a **tremendous desire to do well**, **complete assigned work**, and **succeed** in the area of writing. **(P)**

- _____ **uses computers** as much as possible in order **to make written work more presentable** and easier to read. **(P)**

- _____ writes **simple sentences** revealing **appropriate use of punctuation** and **understanding** of the posed question. **(P)**

- _____ writes using **paragraphs** and **tries** to make **introductions** and **conclusions** effective and **interesting**. **(P)**

- **Some progress was observed**, and _____ is to be commended for his/her **willingness** and **enthusiasm to succeed**. **(P)**

- This has been an area of **very tangible growth** for _____. _____ always **works diligently on improving** his/her writing. **(P)**

- _____ **willingly,** and without asking, **uses a spell checker and other resources to help** him/her **with the correction** of writing errors. **(P)**

- Evidence shows that _____'s **written work has improved** due to **independent, peer**, or **teacher assisted proofreading** and **revision**. **(P)**

- Writing **conventions**, including the **writing process**, need to be **re-taught** next year/term in order to solidify _____'s understanding of writing. **(P)**

- **Many forms of writing were used in class** by _____, including journal, evaluative, newspaper articles, descriptive, letters, observations, predictions, expressing thoughts, opinions, etc. **(P)**

- _____ had **many good ideas** for writing. When he/she writes, **conventions** and **spelling skills** are **usually evident**. **Beginning, middle,** and **end** are beginning to be applied and the **use of paragraphs is developing**. (**P**)

- _____'s **work is always done to the very best of ability** and **displays eagerness** to **follow** our **planning, proofreading,** and **editing routines.** _____'s **writing has improved a great deal** during this past academic year. His/her **ideas are expressed more clearly** and in a **more logical manner.** (**P**)

- _____ has **taken advantage** of some of the **new technologies** available at home and at school in order to help improve **presentation of written text**. To improve ability to **print/write** using pen on paper, _____ is **advised to slow down** and **take** his/her **time**. (**P**)

- _____ is being **trained** to use a **voice recognition software** that will help him/her **put thoughts on paper** in a **well-organized** and **neatly presented** manner. _____ is **encouraged to use** the **home computer** more often **for writing** when **publishing/** completing homework assignments. (**P**)

- _____ **has learned how to take advantage of** available **computer technology**, both at home and at school. **Work submitted** for evaluation is **published** and printed **on the computer, and is often neat** and **well organized.** _____ is **encouraged to slow down** and take his/her time **when handwriting information** or **copying notes** from the blackboard. (**P**)

Positive/Negative

- _____ shows an ability to write in **simple paragraph** form. (**P,N**)

- _____ uses **paragraphs** in writing but still **needs to focus on** more **effective use** of **linking/connecting words**. (**P,N**)

- _____ has **begun to improve** his/her ability to express ideas on paper. **Spelling errors, sentence structure,** and independent **proofreading remain areas of need** and future growth. (**P,N**)

- **Written ideas must be planned, organized in logical order,** and **introduced** and **concluded** effectively. (**P,N**)

- Although _____ **continues** to have **difficulty** with writing, **progress is slowly being made**, and he/she **remains enthusiastic about learning.** (**P,N**)

- _____ has made **some progress in the area of writing conventions**, but **spelling, punctuation,** and **grammar continue to be a great challenge** for him/her. (**P,N**)

- **Organization** of **written content** is **an area of strength** for _____. He/she **writes independently** using **paragraphs** and (often) **organizes ideas** on paper **in ways that are visually pleasing** to the reader. _____ is **encouraged to examine and write about topics** at a **deeper level**. This can be accomplished through careful and patient **planning** and **reflecting before** (prior to) **writing**. (**P,N**)

Report Card and IEP Comments

- _____ **strives to write to the best of** his/her **ability** in class. **To help** him/her with this task he/she has been provided with **access to computers** and **spell checkers**, and **taught prewriting** and **proofreading** strategies. **Writing** is an area that **requires continued attention** for _____. He/she **must carefully proofread** and **edit all work** before it is handed in for marking. **(P,N)**

Negative

- **Written** communication is **difficult** for _____. **(N)**

- _____ 's written work is **short** and **lacks detail**. **(N)**

- _____ continues to have **difficulty** with **penmanship**. **(N)**

- _____ **needs assistance** with **introduction** and **conclusion**. **(N)**

- _____ **writes in paragraph** form **only with** teacher **assistance**. **(N)**

- _____ **needs prompts** and **clues to begin** and continue writing. **(N)**

- **Writing** is an area that **requires continued attention** for _____. **(N)**

- **Journal reflections need to be more numerous** and **better thought out**. **(N)**

- Frequent **distractibility** and **lack of focus** are affecting academic achievement. **(N)**

- **Writing sentences** that accurately express **ideas** is a **challenge** for _____. **(N)**

- _____ **needs assistance** with **organizing information** to **develop** a **central idea**. **(N)**

- _____ found it **difficult** to **organize** and **express researched material** into words. **(N)**

- _____ **often resists teacher effort** to provide instruction and assistance in writing. **(N)**

- **Organizing ideas** into **paragraphs** occurs only with teacher guidance, supervision, and assistance. **(N)**

- _____ often **rushes through work without taking the time to proofread** it adequately. **(N)**

- _____ **writes even single sentences with great difficulty** and considerable assistance. **(N)**

- _____ has **difficulty completing** written assignments without direct supervision. **(N)**

- _____ **must carefully proofread** and **edit all work** that is to be handed in for marking. **(N)**

- _____ **expresses thoughts** and **feelings** about ideas in written form in a **very limited way**. **(N)**

- _____ **forms paragraphs** that contain the **main and** related ideas **in a very limited way**. **(N)**

- _____ 's **written work** (often/usually) **reveals** a **need for a clearer organization of thoughts** and **ideas**. **(N)**

- _____ is able to write a **simple sentence** with **teacher assistance** and **use of technology** (text editing tools). **(N)**

- _____ **has some difficulty brainstorming for ideas** and **organizing information** in a **logical sequence**. **(N)**

- _____ is very **reluctant to produce written work** and has been **offered** a variety of **options** with which to express his/her ideas. **(N)**

- **Further work is needed** to ensure that an **introduction** and **conclusion** are always included, effective, and related to the **main idea**. **(N)**

- **Introduction** and **conclusion** seem **weak** and **simplistic**, and **extensive revision/ correction** of **conventions** is **required**. **(N)**

- _____ **writes** too **quickly**, frequently **not paying enough attention** to the need for effective **planning** and use of **paragraphs**. **(N)**

- _____ **has difficulty** and **requires assistance** with **interpreting** and **expressing researched information** in his/her own words. **(N)**

- _____ **does not always put** forward a **consistent effort** in writing. _____ is (very/ often) **reluctant to produce detailed written work**. **(N)**

- _____ **needs reminders** to write using **paragraphs**. He/she requires teacher assistance with **introduction** and **conclusion** of written work. **(N)**

- **Written work** shows **limited reasoning** by using **some ideas** that are simple, undeveloped, or **inconsistently related** to the purpose of the task. **(N)**

- **Revision** and **proofreading** of work **remain areas of** (significant) **need** for _____ as he/she continues to **struggle with spelling** and **sentence structure**. **(N)**

- **With teacher** or peer **assistance**, _____ **is able** to organize **written information** into **short paragraphs** that include the **main idea** and related **details**. **(N)**

Report Card and IEP Comments

- **Accurate**, (meaningful and thorough) **assessment** of **writing, reading,** and **oral** and visual communication ability **has been hindered** this term by _____'s **frequent absence from school**. **(N)**

- Throughout the term, **much time has been spent assisting** _____ with **penmanship** technique, **physical organization** of **written text, basic punctuation, spelling,** and **grammar**. **(N)**

- _____ **has began to improve** his/her **ability** to **express ideas on paper. Spelling errors, sentence structure,** and independent **proofreading remain** areas of **need** and future growth. **(N)**

- **With much teacher** or **peer assistance,** _____ is able to **organize written information** into **short paragraphs** that include the **main idea** and related **details**. **(N)**

- Writing that has been submitted for evaluation **shows evidence of clear** (straightforward) **main idea**, with **introduction** and **conclusion** that include some effective elements but at times remain **undeveloped**. **(N)**

- _____ **neglected to finish** *any* of the required work for the "_____" unit in spite of daily reminders and opportunities to work in class. The **mark** for writing **is based only on the work** that was **submitted** for evaluation. **(N)**

- _____ **received numerous reminders to correct spelling** and **punctuation errors** in written work. **Much greater effort is needed** in the future if he/she is to reach his/her full potential and experience success in writing. **(N)**

- _____ now routinely writes using **paragraphs, but requires teacher assistance** to ensure that all steps of the **writing process** are adhered to, especially the **prewriting stage** (brainstorming, planning, organizing, and **sequencing** of information). **(N)**

- _____ **needs constant** (continual/ regular/ nonstop) **encouragement to begin and complete writing activities**. It would be advantageous for _____ to use his/her **cursive writing** when copying notes. _____ should continue to practice creating **jot notes** to help him/her **stay on task**. **(N)**

- In _____'s opinion, **only the "draft" copy** of written work **was necessary.** _____ **often submitted assignments without** an independent **effort to correct the convention type of errors**. When questioned, he/she **showed evidence of knowing** the **proofreading** and **editing strategies**. **(N)**

- _____ **does not always put** forward a **consistent effort** in writing. _____ is **(very reluctant) to produce detailed written work**, and has been taught a variety of strategies to use when expressing ideas in written form. **Positive reinforcement** and adult **encouragement** have **enabled** _____ **to complete writing tasks** this term. **(N)**

- **Lack of familiarity with the spelling of often-used words** makes _____'s writing very **difficult to interpret**. _____ **participated** in **individualized exercises** involving (**the study** of **common prefixes** and **consonant blends**). It is **recommended** that _____ **read and write** as often as possible, at home and at school. (**N**)

- _____ **has difficulty** (needs assistance with) **organizing information** to develop a **central idea**. **Introduction** and **conclusion** are (usually/ sometimes) **quite weak** and **simplistic,** and **considerable revision/correction** of **conventions** is **required**. Written work shows inadequate **reasoning** by using some **ideas** that are **simple**, **undeveloped**, or **inconsistently related to** the **purpose** of written work. (**N**)

- It usually **takes** _____ **a long time to begin writing**, and when he/she does, **writing** is often **minimal**. _____'s written pieces are **completed as fast as possible**. To get a higher mark in writing, it is recommended that _____ **expresses** his/her **thoughts** in a **more detailed** and **organized manner**, paying attention to **length** of **sentences** and **correct punctuation**. (**N**)

- _____ **could improve** his/her writing ability by taking the time to ensure that the entire **writing process** is followed (**prewriting**, **drafting**, **editing** and **revising**, and **publishing**). _____ often **gives up on simple tasks, without putting forth** the required amount of **planning** and **effort**. **With assistance,** _____ is able to write a **composition** that includes a relatively **clear main idea. Further work is needed** to ensure that an **introduction** and **conclusion** are always included, effective, and related to the **main idea**. (**N**)

- _____ **struggles to express** original **thoughts** on paper. (**N,N**)

- _____ **expresses thoughts** and **feelings** about ideas in written form in a (very) **limited way**. (**N,N**)

- _____ **writes** even a **single sentence with** (great) **difficulty** and **considerable teacher assistance**. (**N,N**)

- **Proofreading** and **editing stages were** (are) **not always adhered to,** and _____'s **participation** in the writing aspect of our language arts program **was at times minimal**. (**N,N**)

- _____ continues to have (great/much) **difficulty with any written task**. _____ needs to learn to **do a little bit of work at a time** to get through assignments before the deadline. He/she continues to have **difficulty putting** his/her **ideas on paper**. This is compounded by his/her **negative attitude toward writing**, and **learned behaviors of avoidance**. _____ needs to realize that putting forth a concerted effort will eventually pay off. (**N,N**)

Next Steps

- _____ is encouraged to work on **proofreading and editing** of all written work. (**NS**)

- _____ is encouraged to work on the **development** and **organization of ideas** in written work. (**NS**)

- _____ is **encouraged to** work on the **development** and **organization of ideas** in written work. (**NS**)

- _____ is encouraged to **write** as **often** as possible, expressing himself/herself in **different forms of writing.** (**NS**)

Writing Process

General

- The **mark** for writing **is based only on the work that was submitted** for evaluation. **(G)**

- _____ **arranges ideas** into **paragraphs** with (_some/ much/ great deal of_) teacher guidance, supervision, and assistance. **(G)**

- (_With assistance/ Sometimes/ Usually/ Consistently/ Independently_), _____ explains the **main ideas** in written work?, and tells how **details support** them. **(G)**

- (_With assistance/ Occasionally/ Usually,_ _____ communicates **ideas, thoughts, feelings,** and **information** for different **purposes** and to **identified audiences**, using **forms of writing** that are **relevant** and **apporopriate. (G)**

- _____ (_rarely/ sometimes/ usually/ consistently_) **generates**/constructs/organizes and **records ideas** for writing through **discussion/brainstorming**, and **develops** a **good writing plan** (outline, diagram, story map, etc.). This is often done **with** (_much/ some/ little/ no_) **teacher assistance**. (G)

Positive

- _____ **uses** the **stages of writing** to produce **work of high quality**. **(P)**

- **With assistance**, _____ is able to write a (_composition/ essay/ paper_) that includes a relatively/very clear **main idea**. **(P)**

- **Some progress** was **observed**, and _____ is to be commended for his/her **willingness** and **enthusiasm to succeed**. **(P)**

- Writing (**conventions/ rules**), including the **writing process**, need to be **re-taught** next (_year/ term_) in order to solidify _____ 's understanding of writing. **(P)**

- _____ 's **work** is **always done to the** very **best of ability**, and he/she **displays eagerness to follow** our **planning, proofreading,** and **editing routines**. **(P)**

Positive/Negative

- _____ is **encouraged to examine** and **write about topics** at a **deeper level**. This can be accomplished through careful and patient **planning** and **reflecting prior to writing**. **(P,N)**

- _____ **puts a great deal** of **effort into** his/her written **work**. Greater results could be accomplished through **more effective planning** and **editing** of work. **(P,N)**

Negative

- **Writing sentences** that accurately communicate **ideas** is **a challenge** for _____. (**N**)

- _____ is encouraged to make **revision** and **editing** a **routine** part of the writing process. (**N**)

- _____ has **difficulty** with **completing** written assignments without **direct supervision**. (**N**)

- _____ is encouraged to work on the **development** and **organization of ideas** in written work. (**N**)

- _____ **communicates ideas** in written form **with assistance**, using a few of the **conventions** studied. (**N**)

- _____ needs to make **brainstorming** and **organization** of ideas a routine part of every writing activity. (**N**)

- **Written ideas** must be **planned**, **organized** in **meaningful sequence**, and **introduced** and **concluded** effectively. (**N**)

- _____ has **some difficulty brainstorming** for **ideas** and **organizing information** in a way **that makes sense**. (**N**)

- **To** further **improve** in this area, _____ **must make an effort** to develop a **writing plan** (outline, diagram, story map, brainstorm for possible ideas, etc.) as one of the **first steps** of the writing process. (**N**)

- _____ **spends much time** in an **effort to correct** his/her **spelling** errors instead of first organizing the **main idea**. _____ should work **first** on putting his/her **thoughts on paper** and **then editing** what has been written. (**N**)

- _____ now routinely writes using **paragraphs**, but **requires teacher assistance** to ensure that all steps of the **writing process** are adhered to, especially the **prewriting stage** (brainstorming, planning, organizing, and ordering of information). (**N**)

- In _____'s opinion, **only the "draft" copy** of written work **is necessary**. _____ often/usually **submitted assignments without** an independent **effort to correct the convention type of errors**. When questioned, he/she **showed evidence of** knowing/ understanding the **proofreading** and **editing strategies**. (**N**)

- _____ **could improve** his/her **writing ability by taking the time** to ensure that the whole/entire **writing process** is **followed** (prewriting, drafting, editing and revising, and publishing). _____ **often gives up** on **simple tasks, without** putting forth the required amount of **planning** and **effort. With assistance,** _____ is able to write a composition that includes a (relatively) clear **main idea**. (**N**)

- _____ **needs to talk about** his/her **ideas** at length **before** initiating any **written work**. Once he/she has expressed himself/herself **orally**, he/she can begin to recognize **key words** and **concepts** that can aid the **writing process**. _____ **requires intensive support** in this area to be successful. _____ feels more successful in writing when the teacher initially **scribes** for him/her. This helps him/her **organize** his/her **thoughts** and stay on task. _____ has **difficulty** with **completing** written assignments without **direct supervision**. He/she has been given access to a **word processor** for his/her **final draft**. _____ **needs to re-read** his/her work and check for **correct spelling, grammar,** and **punctuation. (N)**

Proofeading and Editing

General

- _____ (*rarely/ sometimes/ usually/ regularly and consistently*) **revises** and **edits** written work. (**G**)

- **Revision** of own written work **is done** (*only with teacher assistance/ with assistance/ with some assistance/ routinely and successfully, without a single reminder*). (**G**)

- _____ (*only with teacher assistance/ with assistance and encouragement/ with some assistance and encouragement/ independently/ routinely*) **uses** the **proofreading checklist** sheet. (**G**)

- _____ **revises** and **edits** personal work using **teacher and peer feedback** (*only with teacher assistance/ with assistance/ independently/ independently, accurately, and effectively*). (**G**)

- Writing **conventions** have been, and continue to be, formally taught. Focus on **high frequency** (often used) **words** and **proofreading** of written work ensures continued **awareness** and need to correct errors. (**G**)

- _____ (*rarely/ with teacher prompts and reminders/ sometimes/usually/ consistently*) proofreads and edits own writing **taking into account peer/teacher recommendation and suggestion** and **using a variety of** available **resources** (editing checklist, spell check, dictionary, thesaurus, other books, etc.). (**G**)

Positive

- _____ **independently proofreads** written work. (**P**)

- _____ **proofreads** written work **effectively** most of the time. (**P**)

- An **improvement** has been **noted** in the areas of **proofreading** and **editing** of work. (**P**)

- _____ **independently revises** and **edits** own work **in collaboration** with others. (**P**)

- _____ **has progressed** in the areas of **proofreading** and **correction of spelling errors**. (**P**)

- **Careful** and **habitual proofreading** of written text **has led to improved written expression**. (**P**)

- **Some progress was observed**, and _____ is to be commended for his/her **willingness** and **enthusiasm to succeed**. (**P**)

- _____ **willingly**, and **without asking**, **uses** a **spell checker** and **other resources** to **help** him/her **with correction of** writing **errors**. (**P**)

- Evidence (test results) shows that _____ 's **written work has improved** due to **independent**, **peer,** or **teacher assisted proofreading** and **revision**. (**P**)

- **Lessons learned** in class **have always been applied** to written work, and _____ is to **be congratulated on** the **consistent effort** in this area. (**P**)

- _____ 's **work** is always **done to the very best of ability,** and he/she **displays eagerness to follow** our **planning, proofreading,** and **editing routines**. (**P**)

- _____ **is beginning** to **proofread** and **correct** his/her **final drafts**. _____ is encouraged to continue to **focus on grammar, punctuation, spelling,** and **style**. (**P**)

- _____ **continues to amaze everyone** with his/her **progress** in writing this term. **Progress occurred** mostly **in terms of volume, better quality of work**, and noted change in **attitude**. (**P**)

Positive/Negative

- _____ **revises** and **edits** work **based on the feedback**/response from the teacher and peers **most of the time**. (**P,N**)

- _____ has **begun to improve** his/her ability to express ideas on paper. **Spelling errors, sentence structure**, and independent **proofreading remain** areas of **need** and future growth. (**P,N**)

- **Proofreading** and **editing do not come naturally** (and are not easy) for _____ but current **effort** is **encouraging**. (**P,N**)

- _____ has made **some progress** in the area of writing conventions, but **spelling, punctuation,** and **grammar** continue to be a **significant challenge**. (**P,N**)

- **Editing** of own work **is a difficult task** for _____, but he/she has been **observed working diligently** on this part of the writing process. (**N,P**)

Negative

- _____ **inconsistently proofreads** and **edits** own work. (**N**)

- _____ **proofreads** work **with assistance** and **reminders**. (**N**)

- _____ still **requires reminders to proofread** his/her written work. (**N**)

- An **improvement** has been **noted** in the areas of proofreading and _____. (**N**)

- **Proofreading** and **editing** of work **must be regular** and habitual if the quality of work is to improve. (**N**)

- _____ **often rushes** through work **without taking the time to proofread** it adequately. (**N**)

- **Regular proofreading** and **editing** of written work **is highly recommended** and encouraged. (**N**)

- _____ **revises** and **edits** personal work **using feedback** from the teacher and peers, **with assistance**. (**N**)

- All **words must be proofread** and **edited** for **spelling errors** in the material that is submitted for evaluation. (**N**)

- Every **effort must be made** to correct spelling errors during the **editing stage** of the writing process. (**N**)

- _____ **needs to re-read** his/her work and check for **correct spelling**, **grammar,** and **punctuation**. (**N**)

- _____ **writes quickly** and **often neglects to plan** and **organize ideas** in **logical sequence**. (**N**)

- _____ **inconsistently revises** his/her own work (using the **spell checker** and alphabetized **word list**). (**N**)

- _____ often **submits assignments without** an independent **effort to correct** the **convention** type of **errors**. (**N**)

- **Proofreading** and **editing stages** are **often skipped** as _____ **habitually refuses** (neglecs) **to correct** written work. (**N**)

- **Editing** of written text (correcting spelling) should be done only after **ideas** have first been **expressed** (written/ recorded) **on paper**. (**N**)

- _____ **must proofread** all personal written text **carefully** and **habitually**. This **will lead to improved written expression**. (**N**)

- **Revision** and **proofreading** of work **remain areas of** (great) **need** for _____ as he/she **continues to struggle** with **spelling** and **sentence structure**. (**N**)

- **Proofreading** and **editing** of written work **seem difficult** for _____ because of the need for **extensive revision/correction** of **conventions** and **grammar**. (**N**)

- **Proofreading** and **editing stages** are not always **adhered to,** and _____'s **participation** in the writing aspect of language arts program is at times **minimal**. (**N**)

- _____ is **encouraged** to **strive toward a more thorough** and **consistent proofreading** and **editing** routine. More time needs to be spent on **memorizing common** and **frequently used words** in order to become a more confident speller. (**N**)

- In _____ 's opinion, **only the "draft" copy** of written work **is necessary**. _____ **often submitted assignments without** an independent **effort to correct** the **convention type of errors**. When questioned, he/she **showed evidence of knowing** (some/ most of) **the proofreading** and **editing strategies**. (**N**)

Next Steps

- _____ is encouraged to make **editing** and **proofreading** of written work a **routine** part of the writing process. (**NS**)

- _____ is encouraged to work on **proofreading and editing** of all written work. (**NS**)

Language Conventions

General

- _____ **shows use** of (*a few/ some/ most/ all*) **basic conventions** (rules of language). (**G**)

- _____ writes (*few/ one or more/ numerous*) **simple sentences** that contain **appropriate and accurate punctuation and grammar**. (**G**)

- _____ (*with assistance/ sometimes/ frequently/ consistently/ effectively and confidently*) **uses correctly** the learned **spelling**, **grammar**, and **punctuation conventions**. (**G**)

- _____ is **encouraged** to make **consistent use of word lists, dictionary, thesaurus,** and other **language tools** while writing and editing his/her work. (**G**)

- _____ (*rarely/ sometimes/ often/ consistently*) **shows** (***grasp/ understanding/ knowledge/Hawareness***) of **spelling, punctuation**, and **grammar** rules. (*Extensive/ Moderate/ Minimal/ No*) **revision** of work is required. (**G**)

- _____ uses (*a few/ at least half/ most/ all*) of the (*learned/ studied/ taught*) **conventions** (*with numerous and frequent errors/ with several minor errors/ with practically no errors/ with no errors*). (**G**)

- _____ has been introduced to the **skills** necessary for writing an **essay** (i.e., **research, introduction, transitions, paragraphs,** and **conclusion**). _____ requires (*much/ some/ little/ no*) assistance while **researching** and **reporting** on a topic. (**G**)

Positive

- _____ writes **simple sentences** showing **appropriate use of punctuation** and **understanding** of the posed question. (**P**)

- _____ uses **advanced conventions** in (stories, personal and daily writing, etc.) **accurately, routinely,** and **confidently**. (**P**)

- **Some progress** was **observed**, and _____ is to be commended for his/her **willingness** and **enthusiasm to succeed**. (**P**)

Positive/Negative

- _____ has made **some progress in the area of writing conventions**, but **spelling, punctuation,** and **grammar continue to be** a (significant) **challenge** for him/her. (**P,N**)

Negative

- _____ **sometimes remembers** to use **capitals** and **periods**, and the **sentence structure** shows **some maturity**. (**N**)

- To get a higher mark in writing, it is recommended that _____ **expresses** his/her **thoughts in** a **more detailed** and **organized manner**, paying attention to **length of sentences** and **correct punctuation**. (**N**)

- _____ **received** assistance and **numerous reminders to correct spelling** and **punctuation errors** in written work. (**Much**) **greater effort is needed** in the future if he/she is to reach his/her full potential and experience success in writing. (**N**)

- Throughout the term, **much time had been spent assisting** _____ with the **penmanship** technique, **physical organization of written text**, **basic punctuation**, **spelling**, and **grammar**. (**N**)

- In _____ 's opinion, **only the "draft" copy** of written work **is necessary**. _____ **often submits assignments without** an independent **effort to correct the convention type of errors**. When questioned, _____ **shows evidence of knowing** the **proofreading** and **editing strategies**. (**N**)

Written Expression

General

- _____ will **need to continue with** his/her **efforts to improve spelling and written expression** if further gains are to be made in area of Language Arts. (**G**)

Positive

- This has been an area of (very) **tangible growth** for _____. _____ always **works diligently on improving** his/her writing. He/she **takes the time to read teacher comments** and **reflect** on what can be done to improve achievement. _____ writes using **paragraphs** and tries to make **introductions** and **conclusions effective** and **interesting**. (**PP**)

- _____ is **beginning to write more elaborate sentences** by using **adjectives** and **adverbs**. (**P**)

- **Careful** and **habitual proofreading** of written text **will lead to improved written expression**. (**P**)

- **Organizing information** to develop a **main idea** is becoming an **easier** task for _____. (**P**)

- **Some progress was observed**, and _____ is to be commended for his/her **willingness** and **enthusiasm to succeed**. (**P**)

- _____ **listens to teacher advice** and **studies** own **writing errors** in order to learn from them. **Careful** and **habitual proofreading** of written text **will lead to improved written expression**. (**P**)

Positive/Negative

- _____ is encouraged to **write** as **often** as possible, expressing himself/herself in **different forms of writing**. (**P,N**)

- _____ is **encouraged to produce shorter pieces of writing** and **focus on quality**, **accuracy**, and **content**. (**P,N**)

- **Amount of** written **output** has **increased**, but _____ **continues to need assistance** with **writing complete sentences** and ensuring that his/her **verb tenses** are **written** with **accuracy**. (**P,N**)

- _____ is **encouraged to examine** and **write about topics at a deeper level**. This can be accomplished through careful and patient **planning** and **reflecting prior to writing**. (**P,N**)

- _____ is noted for **increasing the volume of** his/her **written output**; however, **greater attention** needs to be given to **proofreading, editing,** and **rerision** of **all written work.** _____ **needs to make brainstorming** and **organization** of ideas **a routine part** of every writing activity. **(P,N)**

- _____ is **encouraged to produce writing that focuses on quality, detail, accuracy,** and **content.** _____ **continues to use effectively** our **portable spell checker** to **correct difficult-to-spell words** and **words** that are **difficult to look up/** find **in the dictionary. (P,N)**

- _____ has **improved the quality** of his/her daily writing. He/she **sometimes remembers** to use **capitals** and **periods,** and the **sentence structure** shows **some maturity** (improvement). _____ has **good voice** in his/her writing, and should be encouraged to write a personal **journal** over the summer. **(P,N)**

- **Organization** of **written content** is **an area of strength** for _____. He/she **writes independently** using **paragraphs** and often **organizes ideas** on paper **in ways** that are **visually pleasing.** _____ is **encouraged to examine** and **write about topics at a deeper level.** This may be accomplished through careful and patient **planning** and **reflecting prior to writing. (P,N)**

- _____ **uses computers** in the classroom **to write, edit,** and **publish** written work. _____ has been **working** hard **at improving** writing skills. It is suggested that he/she **always read teacher comments** and **reflect** on what can be done to improve achievement. **Written ideas must be planned, organized** in **proper order,** and **introduced** and **concluded** effectively. **(P,N)**

- _____ **must make an effort** to **carefully** and **habitually proofread** all text in personal writing. This will lead to improved written expression. A **higher degree** of **interest in writing is noted. (N,P)**

Negative

- **Written ideas** must be **planned, organized** in **logical sequence,** and **introduced** and **concluded** effectively. **(N)**

- _____ is encouraged to make **revision** and **editing** a **routine** part of the writing process. **(N)**

- **Proofreading** and **editing** of work **must be regular** and habitual if the quality of work is to improve. **(N)**

- Written **ideas must be introduced** and **concluded effectively** and **organized** in logical sequence. **(N)**

- _____ needs to make **brainstorming** and **organization** of ideas **a routine part** of every writing activity. **(N)**

- _____ **needs to proofread** all personal written text **carefully** and **routinely.** This **will lead to improved written expression. (N)**

- **Further work is needed** to ensure that an **introduction** and **conclusion** are always included, effective, and related to the main idea. (**N**)

- _____ has some **difficulty brainstorming** for ideas and **organizing information** in a way that makes sense (proper order). (**N**)

- Regular, **daily writing** improves **written expression.** _____ is encouraged to **write** as **often** as possible, expressing himself/herself in **different forms of writing.** (**N**)

- _____ **must put greater effort** in expressing himself/herself more **thoroughly** in written form. **Proofreading** and **editing** of work **must become routine** if the quality of work is to improve. (**N**)

- _____ is **learning to organize information** to create a **main idea**. The **introduction** and **conclusion need** some **work,** and **extensive revision/correction** of **conventions** is needed. (**N**)

- _____ has great ideas and is **able** to verbally demonstrate/express complex thoughts and opinions; **however, placing ideas on paper** in a **lengthier** and **more organized way continues to be** (is always) **a struggle**. (**N**)

- _____ is **learning to organize information** to establish a **main idea**. The **introduction** and **conclusion** in everyday, personal writing **need** some **work,** and **extensive revision/correction** of **conventions** is required. (**N**)

- _____ **has difficulty organizing information** to form a **main idea**. The **introduction** and **conclusion** are usually **ineffective** and **simplistic,** and **extensive revision/correction** of **conventions** is **needed**. Written work demonstrates **limited reasoning**, often showing the use of **simple ideas** that are **often unrelated** to the **reason** for writing. (**N**)

- _____ **needs assistance with organizing information** to **form** a **main idea**. The **introduction** and **conclusion** are **usually plain** and **simple,** and **much revision/correction of writing conventions is required**. Writing **shows insufficient reasoning** by often incorporating **simple, undeveloped ideas** that seem unrelated to the main **reason** for writing. (**N**)

- **Performance** in writing is **inconsistent. Introduction** and **conclusion** are **difficult to recognize** but **sometimes show taught** (suggested) **components**. Written **work shows insufficient reasoning** by using **simple ideas,** often **unrelated** to the **reason** for writing. _____ is encouraged to make **revision** and **editing** a **routine** part of the writing process. (**N**)

- _____ has **learned to spell correctly** approximately _____% of the **high frequency** (often used) **words** that were misspelled at the beginning of the year. _____ continues to make simple **spelling errors** in his/her daily writing. _____ is encouraged to make **editing** and **proofreading** of written work a **routine** part of the **writing process**. (**N**)

- _____ still **requires reminders to proofread** his/her written work. He/she **is beginning to use** a **computer** for writing (journals/ paragraphs/ opinions/ short pieces of work), and a **spell checker** to assist with self-correction. Keeping a **journal** of such things as (*feelings, events, and family outings*) over the summer will help reinforce some of the acquired written skills. **(N)**

• _____ **needs** to make a **greater effort to write** using **full sentences.** _____ is **often observed writing as little as possible** of what is expected. **Numerous spelling errors** could be the cause of minimal writing, but he/she is encouraged to overcome this hindrance by simply **taking more chances. Computer editing tools** can be used to help fix the **spelling errors** and free him/her to concentrate on other aspects of writing. **(N)**

• _____ has some **difficulty brainstorming** for ideas and **organizing information** in a way that makes sense. **Introduction** and **conclusion** are **not easy to locate** and have **few**, or **none**, **of the required components/elements.** Written **work shows weak reasoning** through the use of **few simple, undeveloped ideas** that are often **unrelated** to the **reason** for writing. _____ **revises** and **edits** work (**using teacher** and **peer feedback**) **with assistance. (N)**

• _____ **needs to talk about** his/her **ideas** at length **before** initiating any **written work.** Once he/she has expressed himself/herself orally, he/she can begin to recognize key words and concepts that can aid the **writing process.** To be successful, he/she **requires intensive support** in this area. _____ feels more successful in writing when the teacher first **scribes** for him/her. This usually helps with **organizing thoughts** and **staying on task.** _____ has **difficulty completing** writing **assignments** without direct teacher supervision. He/she **needs to re-read** his/her work and check for **spelling, grammar,** and **punctuation** errors. **(N)**

• **Organizing information** to create/compose a **main idea** is a **difficult task** for _____. **Written sentences** are **often broken, short,** and **incomplete. Writing a daily journal at home would help** _____ become more comfortable with the task of writing. **(N,N)**

Spelling

General

- _____ **is encouraged to review** his/her **spelling lists during** _____ in order **to maintain** current **gains**. (**G**)

- _____ will **need to continue with** his/her **effort to improve spelling and written expression** if further gains are to be made in area of Language Arts. (**G**)

- _____ is **able to produce final copies** of written work **that are free of spelling errors** (*with teacher assistance/ with some assistance/ independently/ independently and accurately*). (**G**)

General/Negative

- **Regular**, **daily reading** and **work** at home **on** _____s' **personal high frequency** (often used) **words** list **would help** him/her spell correctly some of these words. (**G,N**)

Positive

- **Spelling remains a huge** and clear **strength** for _____. (**P,P**)

- _____ **shows increasing ability to spell** assigned **word lists** through use of **phonics**. (**P**)

- **Some progress was observed**, and _____ is to be **commended** for his/her **willingness and enthusiasm to succeed**. (**P**)

- _____ 's **ability** to spell words **continues to improve**. _____ is **learning** to **look for spelling patterns** and **use all available tools** to improve spelling. (**P**)

- **Use of electronic** and **computer spell checkers** is **helping** _____ **spell words correctly**, without spending a great deal of time looking for strategies that work. (**P**)

- All **words must be proofread** and **edited** for spelling errors in the work that is submitted for evaluation. _____ has **made progress** in learning how to spell **high frequency words** in class. (**P**)

- _____ **continues to improve** his/her **ability to spell unfamiliar words** through participation in the **high frequency words** remediation program, use of **spelling rules**, and regular **exposure to written text**. (**P**)

- _____ **continues to work diligently to improve** her/his **spelling skills** by **carefully editing** written work and **paying close attention to each misspelled word**. _____ is encouraged to continue to learn how to spell the top (five hundred) **often used words**. (**P**)

- _____ is **learning to look** for **spelling patterns** and use all available **tools** to **improve spelling**. _____ **continues to improve** his/her **ability to spell unfamiliar words** through participation in the **high frequency words** remediation program, use of **spelling rules**, and regular **exposure** to written text. (**P**)

- Regular, **daily reading**, **focus on spelling patterns**, and a **conscious effort to spell words correctly** (especially the personal **high frequency words** list) **would help** _____ create noticeable improvement. In class, _____ **has been using** a **portable** desktop **spell checker** to successfully correct spelling errors. **It is recommended** that _____ get a similar **electronic spell checker** for use **at home**. (**P**)

Positive/Negative

- _____ has made **some progress in the area of writing conventions**, but **spelling, punctuation**, and **grammar continue** to be a **great challenge**. (**P,N**)

- _____ **is learning to edit** his/he own work **by using** a variety of available **tools** (classroom spell checkers, computer, peer editing forms, proofreading checklist, etc.). _____ is to be **commended** for **showing interest** in **handing in**/submitting **work that is free of** spelling and grammatical **errors**. _____ continues to require assistance with this task. (**P,N**)

- Every **effort must be made** to correct every spelling error during the **editing stage** of the writing process. _____ **continues to improve** his/her **ability to decode** unfamiliar words through the **high frequency words remediation** program, **spelling rules**, and regular **exposure** to written text. (**N,P**)

- _____ can **sometimes identify** and **correct misspelled words without assistance. However**, when shown an error, he/she is **developing** an **increasing ability to make independent corrections**. _____ is encouraged to break words into smaller **chunks** to facilitate correct spelling. **Daily reading will assist** with accurate spelling. (**N,P**)

- **Editing** of own work is a **difficult task** for _____, but he/she has been **observed working diligently** on this part of the writing process. **With teacher assistance,** _____ **is able to produce final copies** of written work that are free of spelling errors. _____ **is learning how to use spelling strategies** that help spell unfamiliar words. **Progress has been shown** in learning how to spell **high frequency words** in class. (**N,P**)

Negative

- **Spelling continues to be an area of need** and continued remediation. (**N**)

- **Mastering** the **top 100** (200, 300) **often-used words would help improve** spelling skills and **reduce frustration** in writing. (**N**)

- Spelling errors, **sentence structure**, and independent **proofreading** remain **areas that require attention** and **remediation**. (**N**)

- _____ 's **lack of spelling conventions** at times **interferes with reader's understanding** of the finished product. (**N**)

- _____ is encouraged to continue looking for **familiar patterns** in words, and use the **high frequency word list (booklet)** during writing. (**N**)

- **Revision** and **proofreading** of work **remain areas of great need** for _____ as he/she **continues to struggle** with **spelling** and **sentence structure**. (**N**)

- **Proofreading** and **editing** of written work seems **difficult** for _____ because of the need for **extensive revision/correction of conventions, spelling,** and **grammar**. (**N**)

- Throughout the term, **much time was spent assisting** _____ with **penmanship** technique, **physical organization** of written **text, basic punctuation, spelling,** and **grammar**. (**N**)

- _____ **continues to make simple spelling errors** in his/her writing. Regular, **daily reading** and **working at home** on his/her **personal high frequency words** list **would help** him/her spell correctly some of these words. (**N**)

- _____ **experiences difficulty** with the spelling of **words used most often** in writing. It is important that he/she try to apply **spelling patterns** taught in class and his/her **personal words list** when **editing** written work. (**N**)

- _____ **needs reminders** to at least **try** to **spell misspelled words** using the given strategies, **prior to seeking teacher assistance. All words should** (must) **be spelled correctly** in the **work** that is **submitted** for evaluation. (**N**)

- _____ **received numerous reminders** to **correct spelling and punctuation errors** in written work. **Much greater effort is needed** in the future if he/she is to reach his/her full potential and experience success in writing. (**N**)

- _____ **continues to make simple spelling errors** in his/her writing. **Working at home on high frequency words** and making a **list of words** that have been misspelled **would help** him/her spell correctly (at least) some of these words. (**N**)

- _____ **needs reminders to attempt** to spell misspelled words using the given **strategies** and other available **tools, prior to seeking teacher assistance. All words must be** spelled **correctly** in (all) work that is **submitted** for evaluation. (**N**)

- Correct spelling of **commonly used words** (less frequently used words) **is** still **a challenge** for _____. He/she is **encouraged to continue working** on further development of his/her spelling and grammar skills (for written assignments). (**N**)

- _____ is **encouraged** to **strive toward** a **more thorough** and **consistent proofreading** and **editing** of written work. More time needs to be spent on **memorizing common** and **frequently used words** in order to increase confidence in spelling ability. (**N**)

- _____ will need to place **more emphasis on learning the main spelling strategies** and **word patterns** that help develop spelling skills. Moreover, **working on spelling correctly personal high frequency misspelled word lists** would be a solid step in the right direction. (**N**)

- _____ is **encouraged** to make **consistent use of word lists, dictionaries**, and **similar language tools** when writing and editing his/her work. He/she **needs to memorize common** and **frequently used words in order to apply them confidently** to daily writing. (**N**)

- _____ has **learned to spell correctly** approximately _____% of the **high frequency words** (that were misspelled at the beginning of the year). _____ **continues to make simple spelling errors** in his/her daily writing. _____ is encouraged to make **editing** and **proofreading** of written work a regular part of the writing process. (**N**)

- _____ is **encouraged to look** always **for known patterns** and **associations between sounds** and **symbols** of unfamiliar words. **Editing** of written text (correcting spelling errors) **should be done** only **after ideas** have first been **expressed on paper**. Use of the **high frequency word list (booklet)** is very much encouraged during a writing activity. (**N**)

- **Lack of familiarity** with the **spelling** of **high frequency words** makes _____ 's writing (very) **difficult to interpret**. _____ **participated in individualized exercises** involving the study of **common prefixes** and **consonant blends**. It is recommended that _____ **read and write as often as possible**, at home and at school. (**N**)

- **Spelling words** correctly **continues to be a challenge** for _____. He/she is **beginning to use strategies** that can help him/her become a more independent speller, and **only asks for help** as a **last resort**. _____ is (still) encouraged to continue to look for **familiar patterns** in words, and use the **high frequency word list (booklet)** during writing. (**N**)

- **Spelling** continues to be an **area of difficulty** for _____; however, he/she has been **observed working hard** in class on **editing** and **correcting spelling errors**. It is **recommended** that _____ **take home** his/her **personal list** of **misspelled, often-used words** and **learn to spell** them **correctly**. Continued exposure to written words through **daily reading is highly recommended**. (**N**)

- _____ has **made an attempt** this term to **expand** and further **develop** his/her **creative ideas** for some written assignments. He/she **still experiences a lot of** (much/ continued/ significant) **difficulty** with spelling correctly (*some/ many*) **commonly used words** in writing. He/she is encouraged (to continue) to try to apply some of the **spelling patterns** and **rules** taught in class to his/her own writing pieces. (**N**)

- _____ is **encouraged to use** his/her (portable/ classroom/ computer) **spell checker** at all times in order **to correct** the spelling of **unfamiliar words**. _____ needs to make an **accurate connection between** the **sound** and **symbol of individual or groups of letters**, and **remember** that **many words have** the **same** or similar **spelling patterns**. _____ is encouraged to **work on spelling correctly** (at home) his/her **high frequency misspelled word list**. (**N**)

Report Card and IEP Comments

- _____ is (often) **unwilling to participate** fully in our regular **writing and spelling activities.** When he/she does, the **effort is often** (usually) **minimal**, requiring a lot of reminders, prompting, and teacher encouragement. **(N,N)**

- _____ **needs non stop encouragement to begin** writing assignments. Once on task, he/she usually **rushes** through work. _____ often **completes assignments without following instructions**. Further, he/she **does not take** the **time to review** and **edit** written work. _____ **needs to remember** to **apply the spelling strategies** being practiced in class to all written work. **(N,N)**

Reading

General

- _____ **reads** assigned materials (*only with teacher assistance/ with some teacher assistance/ independently and confidently*). (**G**)

- _____ correctly **describes** (retells) (*few/ some/ most/ all*) of the **facts, ideas, events, details,** and **information**. (**G**)

- _____ (*only with teacher assistance/ with some assistance/ independently and confidently*) **selects and reads** appropriate-level **reading material**. (**G**)

- _____ (*rarely/ with frequent reminders/ sometimes/ frequently and eagerly*) **reads materials of** specific **interest** to him/her in class. (**G**)

- Steady **exposure to written words** has increased _____'s repertoire of **decoding** strategies and, therefore, improved **reading comprehension**. (**G**)

- _____ **selects books** for reading during our quiet reading sessions (*only with teacher assistance/ with some teacher assistance/ independently*). (**G**)

- _____ is able to **communicate** his/her **understanding** of written work, showing adequate **supporting evidence** from the work and his/her **own knowledge** (experience) (*only with teacher assistance/ with assistance/ with some assistance/ independently*). (**G**)

Positive

- _____ **reads willingly** during class. (**P**)

- _____ shows evidence of **improved word recognition**. (**P**)

- _____ **chooses** to read **material from a variety of sources**. (**P**)

- _____ **reads with fluency** and (*good/ excellent/ exceptional*) comprehension. (**P**)

- _____ **demonstrates** (shows) **knowledge of phonics** and the ability to apply it to reading of text. (**P**)

- _____ **reads** a variety of **novels at** his/her **functioning level independently**, and (*often/ always/ usually*) chooses **appropriate** reading material. (**P**)

- **Some progress was observed,** and _____ is to be commended for his/her **willingness** and **enthusiasm to succeed**. (**P**)

- _____ **is able to read independently, using phonics** and **other taught** strategies when faced with **unfamiliar words**. (**P**)

- _____ **has gained additional confidence** in his/her reading **by participating in** our **repeated reading program**. His/her **reading speed** and **quality of enunciation have** (definitely/ clearly) **improved**. (**P**)

- _____ **continued to show interest in reading** throughout the term. He/she **read books** and **magazines** from our class collection, as well as **age-appropriate novels** that were signed out from the local **public** (school) **library**. (**P**)

- _____ **participated actively during our repeated reading sessions** as he/she found the selected articles interesting and amusing to read. _____ is **to be commended for** his/her **willingness** to **read aloud** in class. **Reading ability continues to be** (very much) a **strength** for _____. (**P**)

- _____ 's **reading repertoire is quite varied**. He/she **can be found reading** books and other printed materials **throughout the day**, and even keeps several of them inside the desk. _____ **has read from** (textbooks, newspapers, fiction novels, technical manuals, Asterix and Obelix comic series, comic books, computer newspapers, etc.). (**P**)

- _____ **reads regularly in class** and (always) **volunteers to read aloud** to his/her classmates. **Repeated reading** exercises, regular **study of words, word patterns,** and **teacher assisted reading** are **helping** _____ make **tangible progress** in reading **fluency**. _____ is encouraged to **read daily** in order to maintain this progress. (**P**)

Positive/Negative

- _____ 's ability to **understand** (comprehend) **what is being read** continues to improve as he/she learns more about the way **conventions** of written materials are used. Regular **reading at home is** (highly/ definitely/ strongly) **recommended**. (**N,P**)

- _____ continues to **read with difficulty, but progress is** being **made** in **small steps**. (**N,P**)

- _____ **comprehends** at a higher level **when** the **text is read** to him/her (**by others**). (**N,P**)

Negative

- A **novel**, for **independent quiet reading, was brought** to school **only after numerous** teacher **requests** and **reminders**. (**N**)

- _____ **is becoming more aware of word patterns** and their usefulness in **word recognition** and **decoding** of words. (**N**)

- _____ **selects books** for reading during our quiet reading class (only) **with teacher assistance**, as he/she tends to move from book to book **without spending much time reading any of them**. (**N**)

- _____ is a **slow** and **methodical reader**. He/she is **encouraged to read regularly** in order to improve his/her **fluency** and **word recognition**. Some explanations are necessary for a better comprehension (understanding). (**N**)

- _____ 's **ability** to **understand** (comprehend) **what is being read** continues to improve as he/she learns more about the way **conventions** of written materials are used. **To improve reading fluency** and confidence, it is recommended that _____ **read regularly at home**. (**N**)

- _____ continued to **require significant assistance** in the **monitoring** and **completion** of **reading assignments**. _____ has read a variety of books, and has been given opportunities to identify **elements of a story** while explaining how they relate to one another. He/she is encouraged to maintain his/her **reading records** and **read more** on his/her own. (**N**)

- _____ , **with assistance**, is able to **explain** his/her **interpretation** of a written work, showing supporting **evidence**, and from his/her own knowledge and experience. He/she is able to explain **the main idea** in nonfiction material and communicate how individual **details support the main idea** (only with) **with teacher support** (and **prompts**). _____ is encouraged to read every night. (**N**)

General for When Regular, Daily Reading Is Recommended

- Regular **reading at home is recommended**. (**G**)

- _____ is **encouraged to read** every night. (**G**)

- _____ is **encouraged to read** nightly **for pleasure**. (**G**)

- _____ is encouraged to **read daily** in order **to maintain** progress. (**G**)

- **Regular** daily **reading** at **home** is **highly recommended** and encouraged. (**G**)

- **Regular, daily reading at home** (_____ minutes) for interest **will help** improve decoding skills. (**G**)

- _____ is (strongly) **encouraged** to make **daily reading** a regular practice **at home**. (**G**)

- It is recommended that _____ **read** and **write as often as possible**, at home and at school. (**G**)

- **Regular reading** (aloud) **at home is recommended** to help improve reading fluency and comprehension. (**G**)

- Quiet, uninterrupted, **daily reading** at home **is recommended** to improve reading fluency and comprehension. (**G**)

- **To improve reading fluency** and confidence, it is recommended that _____ reads daily (regularly/ at home). (**G**)

- **Regular silent and uninterrupted reading at home is recommended** to improve reading fluency and comprehension. (**G**)

- Reading **aloud** (**regularly**, and quietly) **at home** is recommended to help improve reading **fluency** and **comprehension**. (**G**)

- **Daily** (frequent/ regular) **reading** at home **is highly recommended** as it increases familiarity with and exposure to new words. (**G**)

- **Daily**, **regular reading at home**, throughout the school year, **is highly recommended** as it helps _____ maintain and improve reading skills. (**G**)

- **Daily reading at home**, including the provided **repeated reading exercises**, would help _____ **gain confidence** and improve **decoding skills**. (**G**)

Reading Comprehension

General

- _____ correctly **describes/ shares/ tetells** (*few/ some/ most/ all*) of the **facts**, **ideas**, **events,** and/or **details**. (**G**)

- _____ (*rarely/ with teacher assistance/ sometimes/ usually/ always*) **describes the main** idea (important ideas) in a (*story/ novel/ newspaper article, etc*). (**G**)

- _____ is able to **describe** the **main idea** in writing, and give the required **supporting detail** (*with assistance/ with some clarity and precision/ most of the time/ accurately, precisely, and confidently*). (**G**)

- _____ **is able to name/explain elements** of a story, and **explain** how they **relate** (*only with teacher assistance/ with some assistance/ independently/ independently/ precisely, and confidently*). (**G**)

- **Main idea** and **order of ideas** are **understood accurately** (*some of the time/ most of the time/always*). (**G**)

- _____ **understands** what has been read through the use of **strategies** (*with much/ some/ little*) success and (*much/ some/ no*) assistance. (**G**)

- Continual (regular) **exposure** to **written words increases** the **repertoire** of **decoding strategies** and improves **reading comprehension**. (**G**)

- _____ (*with teacher assistance/ sometimes/ usually/ consistently/ independently*) **answer questions about the main ideas** in _____ , and **describes how** the given **details support** the main idea. (**G**)

- _____ (*with teacher assistance/ with some assistance/ independently, independently/ and accurately*) **retells**, **reflects,** and **relates** read textual (printed) information. (**G**)

- _____ (*rarely/ sometimes/ often/ usually/ always*) **compares/contrasts** events, characters, and/or ideas from the text **to personal experiences**, relationships, feelings, or acquired knowledge. This is an **area of strength** and **growth** for _____. (**G**)

General/Negative

- _____ **should** (must) **read regularly during the summer**, and **discuss** his/her understanding of what he/she has read with an adult. (**G,N**)

- Continual **exposure to written words** increases _____s' **repertoire** of **decoding** strategies and improves **reading comprehension**. (**G,N**)

- _____ **is encouraged to review** his/her **spelling lists during the summer** in order to maintain recent gains. A larger **sight vocabulary** would contribute to improved **fluency** and **comprehension**. _____ **should read regularly** (during the summer) and **discuss** his/her understanding of what has been read with another person. (**G,N**)

- _____ **decodes** unfamiliar words through the use of **strategies** (*with much/ some/ little*) success and (*much/ some/ no*) assistance. **Daily reading** at home **is highly recommended** as it **increases familiarity** with and **exposure to new words**. Continual (regular) **exposure to written words** increases the **repertoire** of **decoding** strategies and is likely to improve **reading comprehension**. (**G,N**)

Positive

- _____ **retells** personal experiences **with passion**, **enthusiasm**, and **clarity**. (**P,P**)

- _____ is **to be congratulated on a greatly improved ability to use reading strategies** to **comprehend** written passages. _____ **always volunteers** to **retell** a story to class, and is **becoming well recognized** by his/her peers for **doing a thorough** and **detailed job**. (**P,P**)

- _____ has **benefited from pre-** and **post**-reading **discussion**. (**P**)

- _____ reads **with fluency** and **comprehension**. (**P**)

- _____ has been **developing confidence** in his/her reading. (**P**)

- **Improvement has been noted** in _____'s **ability to comprehend** what he/she is reading. (**P**)

- _____ **enjoys reading** and **cheerfully volunteers to retell**, **relate**, and **reflect** reading passages. (**P**)

- _____ **is learning to consult the text** or **re-read** passages to find the answer to comprehension questions. (**P**)

- **When questioned,** _____ responds with an **appropriate answer, showing evidence of understanding.** (**P**)

- _____ is **learning to apply reading strategies** such as **imaging** to help him/her improve reading comprehension. (**P**)

- **Some progress** was **observed**, and _____ is **to be commended** for his/her **willingness** and **enthusiasm to succeed.** (**P**)

- _____ **participates well in all reading activities** designed to improve reading **comprehension** and teach **decoding** skills. (**P**)

- **Use of** a variety of **reading strategies** (*before, during, and after reading*) **are helping** _____ **improve** reading **comprehension.** (**P**)

- _____ **always volunteers to retell** a story, and is **becoming well recognized** by his/her peers for doing a **thorough** and **detailed job**. (**P**)

- _____ **participates willingly** in our class reading activities (*reading aloud, repeated reading, reading strategies sessions*) and **continues to make steady progress** in this area. (**P**)

- **Use of a** variety of **reading strategies** (*before, during, and after reading*) are **helping** _____ **improve** reading **comprehension**. _____ **enjoys reading** and **cheerfully volunteers** to **retell**, **relate**, and **reflect** reading passages. (**P**)

- _____'s **ability** to **understand** what has been read **continues to improve** as he/she learns more about the way **conventions** of written materials are used. **To improve reading fluency** and confidence, it is recommended that _____ read daily. (**P**)

- _____ **is learning to apply reading strategies**, such as **imaging**, to help him/her improve reading comprehension. **Daily reading for pleasure**, at home, is **still highly recommended** as it increases familiarity with and exposure to new words. (**P**)

- _____ **is to be commended** for greatly **improved ability** to use **reading strategies** as a way of **comprehending** written passages. _____ **always volunteers to retell** a story to the class, and is **becoming well recognized** by his/her peers for doing a **thorough** and **detailed job**. (**P**)

- _____ has been **developing confidence** in reading. He/she **often volunteers to read aloud** during class discussions. _____ needs to **practice** the **reading strategies** learned in class when he/she reads. _____ is also **encouraged to read for pleasure as often as possible** (every night/ on daily basis). (**P**)

- _____ **continues to develop confidence in** his/her **reading**. He/she **uses a variety of reading strategies** (before, during, and after reading) to help him/her improve reading comprehension. _____ **enjoys reading** and **cheerfully volunteers to retell, relate,** and **reflect** reading passages. Daily, **regular reading at home** is **highly recommended**. (**P**)

Positive/Negative

- _____ **reads** (quite) **effectively**, but **interpreting what has been read**, and outlining/showing **evidence** in support, **are often a challenge**. (**P,N**)

- _____ is **able to comprehend** reading material with success, **if** and **when it is read, studied,** and **discussed together** with the rest of the class. (**P,N**)

- _____ **participates willingly** in our class reading activities (*reading aloud, repeated reading, reading strategies sessions*) and **continues to make steady progress** (in this area). _____ is **able to comprehend** reading material with success, **if** and **when it is read, studied,** and **discussed together** with the rest of the class. (**P,N**)

- _____ **always volunteers to read aloud** (in class) and often **participates with enthusiasm**. When **reading aloud,** _____ is **encouraged to adjust** his/her **reading**

speed according to the **purpose** or **difficulty** of written text. Error-free **decoding** of words will lead to improved comprehension. (**P,N**)

- _____ **participates willingly** in our class reading activities (*reading aloud, repeated reading, reading strategies sessions*) and **continues to make steady progress** (in this area). _____ is **able to comprehend** reading material with success, **if** and **when it is read**, **studied**, and **discussed together** with the rest of the class. (**P,N**)

- **Improvement is noted** in _____'s **ability to comprehend** what he/she is reading. _____ **benefits from pre-**and **post-** reading **discussions**. He/she **is learning to examine** the **text**, or **re-read** passages to find answers to comprehension questions. _____ **requires further practice** with **answering** the "**why**" and **inferential** type of **questions**. **Continued opportunities to retell** read content **in proper** (correct) **order** would be **beneficial**. (**P,N**)

- _____ **struggles reading through** books, but demonstrates a **good understanding** of **content** and **perspective**. (**N,P**)

- _____ **participated** in all reading activities **at the grade** ____ level **with some accommodations**. He/she **struggled reading through** books, but demonstrated a **good understanding** of **content** and **perspective**. (**N,P**)

- _____ **Is able to identify elements** of a story and **explain** how they **relate, with assistance**. He/she can **sometimes identify the main** idea and **is beginning** to make **predictions** based on evidence from the text. (**N,P**)

- _____ **continues to need to read** and **re-read** the story in order **to understand** the **main ideas**. He/she needs to be able to put **ideas** into **paragraphs**, without retelling the entire story. His/her **oral reading skills** are **good** at this level and he/she usually puts forth an **effort** to **read with expression**. (**N,P**)

Negative

- **Weak** (below level) **decoding skills** are making comprehension more difficult. (**N**)

- _____ **participates** in reading activities **with some accommodations**. (**N**)

- A **larger sight vocabulary would contribute** to improved **fluency** and comprehension. (**N**)

- _____ **continues to need to read** and **re-read** (stories) in order **to understand** the **main idea**. (**N**)

- **Continued opportunities to retell** what he/she has read, **in proper order**, **would be of benefit**. (**N**)

- _____ **requires further practice with answering** the "**why**" and **inferential** type of **questions**. (**N**)

- _____ needs to be able to **answer comprehension question/s without retelling** the **entire story**. **(N)**

- _____ **expresses thoughts** and **feelings** based on **read information using** mostly **single-word answers**. **(N)**

- _____ **participated** in all (of our) reading activities **at the grade** ___ level (**with some accommodations**). **(N)**

- **Further work** in use of **spelling patterns** and **word sound cues** is needed **to help make meaning** from printed text. **(N)**

- **Interpreting what has been read**, and **finding supporting evidence**, continue to be (are often) a **challenge** for _____. **(N)**

- **Slow progress** is being made, **but** _____ **can** (will) **continue** to **improve** with **daily reading at home** and continual (regular/ daily) **exposure to printed text**. **(N)**

- _____ is **encouraged to integrate** (use/ combine) **several reading strategy systems** (graphophonic, semantic, syntactic) **in order to make sense** of what is being read. **(N)**

- _____ is **able to understand** reading material with (a great deal of) success **when it is read**, **studied**, and **discussed** together **with the rest of the class**. **(N)**

- _____ is **receiving regular** teacher **assistance to** help him/her **decode** written text and **develop reading strategies** that improve reading comprehension. **(N)**

- _____ continues to **decode unfamiliar words** through the use of **strategies, with some success** and **assistance**. Daily, regular **reading at home**, throughout the school year, **is highly recommended,** as it is likely to help _____ maintain and improve reading skills. **(N)**

- **Improved decoding skills** would (also) **help improve** _____'s **reading comprehension** skills. _____ is still **encouraged** to **read in class with purpose** and **higher level of concentration**. **Daily reading for pleasure**, at home, is (highly) recommended as it increases familiarity with and exposure to new words. It is (also) **recommended** that he/she **carry to class** (daily) **reading material** of interest. **(N)**

- _____ is **receiving consistent** teacher **assistance** to help him/her **decode** written text and **develop reading strategies** that improve reading comprehension. _____, a **computer program**, has **made the reading of more difficult text easier** for _____. **Weak decoding skills** are making **comprehension** more difficult. _____ is **strongly encouraged** to make **daily reading** a regular practice **at home**. **(N)**

Decoding Strategies

General

- _____ **decodes** unfamiliar words by using learned **strategies** with (*much/ some/ little*) success and (*much/ some/ hardly any/ no*) assistance. (**G**)

- Continual **exposure to written words increases** _____ 's **repertoire** of **decoding strategies** and improves **reading comprehension**. **Regular exposure** to written text is (*strongly/highly*) recommended. (**G**)

- _____ is encouraged to continue **using variety of strategies** (identifying word families, using context clues, and sounding out words) to improve his/her decoding skills. **Regular reading** for interest **will** (*definitely/ likely*) **help** in this area. (**G**)

General/Negative

- _____ **reads** unfamiliar words using learned **strategies** *with* (*much/ some/ little*) success and assistance. **Daily reading** at home is highly recommended as it increases (helps increase) familiarity with and exposure to new words. Continual **exposure to written words increases** _____ 's **repertoire** of **decoding strategies** and **improves reading comprehension**. (**G,N**)

Positive

- _____ **reads effectively** and with enthusiasm. (**P**)

- _____ is **beginning to recognize sound** and **word patterns**. (**P**)

- _____ is to be **commended** for being an **enthusiastic reader**. (**P**)

- _____ **attempts to read independently** and **aloud** during class. (**P**)

- _____ **uses picture clues** and **phonics** to **decode unfamiliar vocabulary**. (**P**)

- _____ is **starting to demonstrate some confidence** in his/her reading ability. (**P**)

- **Continued daily reading will improve** _____ 's **ability to decode** written words. (**P**)

- _____ is **becoming more aware** of **word patterns** and their usefulness in word recognition. (**P**)

- Continual **exposure to printed words has increased** _____ 's **repertoire of decoding strategies**. (**P**)

- _____ (*usually/ without any assistance/ always*) **recognizes** and **reads commonly used words**. (**P**)

- _____ is a **very enthusiastic reader** who is **improving** his/her **reading strategies** at a **fast pace**. (**P**)

- _____ **reads aloud confidently**, and is learning to apply **cueing strategies** to improve **decoding** of words. (**P**)

- _____ (usually) **identifies** and **decodes unfamiliar words** by using **common sound, form**, and **spelling patterns**. (**P**)

- **Some progress** was **observed**, and _____ is **to be commended** for his/her **willingness** and **enthusiasm to succeed**. (**P**)

- _____ has **made attempts** to **apply** some of the **phonics** and **word**/spelling **pattern techniques** to reading **difficult words**. (**P**)

- _____ is **encouraged to try** to **decode words on** his/her **own, remembering to apply** the **strategies** learned during our reading class. (**P**)

- _____ **participates well** (effectively) **in all reading activities** designed to improve reading **comprehension** and teach **decoding skills**. (**P**)

- _____ **volunteers to read aloud more often**, and this is **beginning to have a positive effect on** his/her **ability to decode unfamiliar words**. (**P**)

- _____ **continues to improve** his/her ability to decode unfamiliar words **through frequent reading** of a variety of materials and study of **learned word patterns**. (**P**)

- _____ has shown **solid improvement** in this area as he/she has been observed **decoding words** with more **confidence, better accuracy**, and a **louder tone of voice**. (**P**)

- _____'s **ability to decode words continues to improve** as he/she works through the **repeated reading exercises** and **applies** the **taught word patterns** to his/her reading. (**P**)

- _____ **continues to improve** his/her **decoding skills. In spite of** some **errors**, he/she **volunteers to read aloud, usually reading** with **confidence** and **motivation**. (**P**)

- Continued **emphasis on regular reading, study of word patterns**, and familiar **suffixes** is **helping** _____ **improve** his/her decoding skills. Regular, **daily reading** at home is (still) **highly encouraged**. (**P**)

- _____ is to **be congratulated** on **working diligently** to improve decoding skills. _____ **often volunteers** to **read in class** and, in spite of some errors, he/she **continues** to **show motivation** and a **desire to participate** and **improve**. (**P**)

- _____ is **to be congratulated for improving** (noticeably) in this area. In spite of some errors, _____ (usually) **reads with confidence** and **motivation. Continued daily reading will** likely **improve** _____'s **ability to decode** written words. (**P**)

- _____ **continues to improve** (with great strides) in this area. He/she **always volunteers to read aloud** (in class) and **actively participates in** (all) **group reading activities.** _____ 's ability to **decode unfamiliar words** has **noticeably improved** this term (year). (**P**)

- _____ **continues to show enthusiasm** for reading, as he/she often **expresses** a **desire to read aloud** in class. _____ is **learning to apply** his/her **knowledge of word patterns** and **familiar suffixes** to help improve his/her decoding skills. Thank you for your effort _____! (**P**)

- _____ is **starting to demonstrate more confidence** in his/her reading. **With encouragement,** _____ **attempts to read independently** and **aloud** during class. _____ is **encouraged to attempt decoding words on** his/her **own, remembering to apply** the **strategies** learned during the reading class. (**P**)

- _____ **continues to improve** his/her ability to decode unfamiliar words **through frequent reading** of a variety of materials and study of **familiar word patterns.** Continual **exposure to printed words** has **increased** _____ 's **repertoire of decoding strategies** and is (clearly) **improving** his/her ability to **comprehend** written text. (**P**)

- _____ **uses picture/drawing clues** and **phonics to decode unfamiliar words.** He/she **continues to learn other strategies,** such as using **context cues.** _____ is **starting to re-read passages** that do not make sense. He/she is **beginning to recognize sound** and **word patterns.** Continued daily reading, especially over the summer, is encouraged. (**P**)

- _____ is **encouraged to continue using a variety of strategies** (identifying word families, using context clues, and sounding out words) to improve his/her decoding skills. **Regular reading** for interest **would help** in this area. _____ **is showing growth** in area of **vocabulary.** When encountering unfamiliar words, and in order to improve vocabulary, _____ is always encouraged to find and use a **dictionary.** (**P**)

- This has been an area of (tremendous/ noticeable/ much) **growth** for _____. _____ now **reads** _____ **aloud with very few mistakes.** _____ is **to be congratulated** for his/her **effort** and **achievement** in improving decoding strategies. It is recommended that _____ **continue to read daily at home** in order **to maintain** and **improve decoding skills.** (**P**)

- **To improve word recognition,** it is important that he/she stop, think, and **remember some of the decoding strategies** taught in class, prior to seeking teacher assistance. **Daily reading at home,** including the provided (repeated reading) **exercises,** will help _____ **gain confidence** and improve performance in this area. _____ is **to be applauded/**commended **for** his/her **effort** and **excellent attitude** in class. (**P**)

Positive/Negative

- _____ is **to be congratulated for improving noticeably** (in this area). In **spite of** some **errors,** _____ (*usually/ always*) **reads with confidence** and **motivation.** **Continued daily reading** is leading toward improvement in _____ 's ability to decode written words. (**P,N**)

- _____ is starting to demonstrate (some) **confidence** in his/her **reading**. **With encouragement,** _____ **attempts to read independently** and **aloud** during class. _____ **needs to try** to **decode words consistently, remembering to apply strategies** learned in class to reading unfamiliar text. (**P,N**)

- _____ **has shown increased interest in reading.** _____ **volunteers** to **read aloud** during class reading sessions. _____ **needs to make an attempt to decode** words **consistently, remembering to apply the** (learned) **reading strategies.** _____ is **strongly encouraged** to make **daily reading** a regular practice/routine **at home.** (**P,N**)

- **With some** teacher **assistance,** _____ is **learning to recognize** and **pay attention to specific decoding strategies** that help improve decoding, and even spelling skills. _____ **volunteers to read aloud** more **often,** and this is **beginning** to have a **positive effect on** his/her **ability to decode unfamiliar words**. _____ is encouraged to read daily. (**P,N**)

- _____ continued with a **diligent effort** to improve his/her decoding skills this term. _____ **participated well** in all reading activities designed to improve reading **comprehension** and teach **decoding** skills. **Slow progress** is being made, but daily reading at home, and continual **exposure** to printed text, will help _____ improve achievement. _____ is to be applauded for his/her **effort** and **excellent attitude** during class. (**P,N**)

- _____ is **encouraged to continue using a variety of strategies** (identifying word families, using context clues, and sounding out words) to improve his/her decoding skills. **Regular reading for interest** would help with this task. _____ is **showing improvement in** the **area** of **vocabulary growth.** _____ is **encouraged to use** a **dictionary** when unsure of a **word's meaning,** and as a way to enhance personal **vocabulary.** (**P,N**)

- _____ usually **identifies** and **decodes unfamiliar words** by using **common sound, form,** and **spelling patterns**. He/she usually **recognizes often-used words**. He/she is **encouraged to integrate different reading strategies** (use of phonics, previous knowledge, sentence structure) in order to **make sense** of what is being read. **Daily reading** (aloud) at home is recommended to improve reading **fluency**. (**P,N**)

- **With some** teacher **assistance,** _____ is **learning to recognize and pay attention to specific decoding strategies** that help improve decoding, and even **spelling** skills. (**N,P**)

- **Further work is needed** in use of **spelling patterns** and **word sound cues** to **help make meaning** from printed text. **Daily reading** at home, **phonics,** and **repeated reading exercises** are **recommended** to help _____ gain **confidence** and **improve performance** in this area. _____ **continues to exhibit great effort** and (*superb/ great/ exemplary*) **attitude** in class. (**N,P**)

Negative

- **Weak decoding skills** are making **comprehension** (*more/very*) difficult for _____. (**N**)

- _____, a **computer program, has made** the **reading** of more **difficult text easier** for _____. (**N**)

Copyright © 2001, 2003, 2009 by Stevan Krajnjan

- **Interpreting** what has been read and **finding supporting evidence** continue to be **challenges** for _____. **(N)**

- _____ (continues to **decode**) decodes unfamiliar words **through** the use of **strategies** with **some success** and assistance. **(N)**

- _____ **needs to make** a **consistent effort** and **remember** to **apply** the **learned strategies during** the **reading** and **decoding of words**. **(N)**

- _____ **does not always participate** in our class reading activities (reading aloud) and is making **slow progress** in this area. **(N)**

- _____ is **encouraged to integrate** (mix/use) **several cueing systems** in order **to make sense** of what he/she reads (is being read). **(N)**

- _____ is **encouraged to attempt to decode words on** his/her **own, remembering** to **apply** the **strategies** learned in class. **(N)**

- **Slow progress** is being made, **but** _____ **can continue** to **improve** with **daily reading** at home and steady **exposure** to printed text. **(N)**

- _____ is **receiving regular** teacher **assistance to** help him/her **decode** written text and **develop reading strategies** that improve **comprehension**. **(N)**

- _____ is **encouraged to continue using a variety of strategies** (identifying word families, using context clues, and sounding out words) to improve his/her **decoding** skills. **(N)**

- Prior to seeking teacher assistance (and in order **to improve word recognition**), it is important that _____ stop, think, and **remember** some of the **decoding strategies** that have been taught in class. **(N)**

- _____ continues to **decode** unfamiliar words **through the use of strategies** with **some success** and assistance. **Daily,** regular **reading** at home (during the summer months) is **highly recommended,** as it will help _____ **maintain** and improve reading skills. **(N)**

- _____ **needs to show** a **more consistent effort** in **decoding words**, and **remembering to apply** the **strategies** learned in class. Quiet, uninterrupted, **daily reading** at home **is recommended** to improve **decoding** skills, reading **fluency,** and **comprehension**. **(N)**

- _____ is **to be commended** for being an **enthusiastic reader**. He/she **reads aloud without reservation** and is learning to apply **cueing strategies** to improve decoding of words. _____ is **encouraged to continue to read regularly** (and daily at home) in order to improve reading fluency. **(N)**

- _____ **does not always participate** in our class reading activities and is making **slow progress** in this area. _____ is **able to comprehend** reading material with a great deal of success **when it is read**, **studied**, and **discussed with the rest of the class**. _____ is strongly encouraged to make **daily reading** a regular practice **at home**. **(N)**

Report Card and IEP Comments

- **Inability to focus in class** is **currently** making it **difficult** for _____ **to improve** his/her decoding skills. (**N,N**)

- _____ **has shown very little interest** in **reading** during school hours. Quiet **reading sessions** and other reading activities **are often verbally** and **abruptly interrupted** by _____. **Very little progress** is **possible** in this area **unless** _____ **begins to abide by** (follow) **the school's code of conduct**. (**N,N**)

- **To improve** in reading, _____ **needs to become involved in regular, daily reading** at home (___ minutes a day). **Being able to decode** and identify unfamiliar words through recognition of word patterns **requires patience** and a **desire to learn** and **improve**. (**N,N**)

Reading Fluency

General

- _____'s reading **fluency** (*has improved/ is improving/ continues to improve*). (**G**)

Positive

- _____ **reads effectively** and **with enthusiasm**. (**P**)

- _____ reads **with fluency** and **comprehension**. (**P**)

- _____ shows evidence of **increased reading speed**. (**P**)

- _____ shows evidence of **improved word recognition**. (**P**)

- _____ **reads with fluency** and (*good/ excellent*) **comprehension**. (**P**)

- _____'s **oral reading skills** are **good** at this level, and he/she **tries** to **read with expression**. (**P**)

- _____ **has made attempts to apply** some of the **phonics techniques** to reading **difficult words**. (**P**)

- _____ **demonstrates knowledge of phonics** and the ability to **apply** it **to reading** (of written words). (**P**)

- _____ shows **improved fluency** in reading. **Repeated reading** strategies and study of **word patterns** seem to be **helping**. (**P**)

- **Some progress** was **observed**, and _____ is to be commended for his/her **willingness** and **enthusiasm to succeed** in area of reading fluency. (**P**)

- **Repeated reading** exercises, regular **study of words**, **word patterns**, and **teacher assisted reading** have been very **helpful** in improving _____'s **reading fluency**. (**P**)

- _____ has **gained additional confidence** in his/her reading **by taking part in** our **repeated reading program**. His/her **reading speed** and **quality** of **enunciation** have **improved**. (**P**)

- Regular **study of words** and **teacher assisted reading** have helped _____ make **tangible progress** in reading **fluency**. _____ is encouraged to **read daily** in order **to maintain** this **progress**. (**P**)

- _____'s **ability to make meaning of print continues to improve** as he/she learns more about the way **conventions** of written materials are used. **To improve reading fluency** and confidence, it is recommended that _____ read daily. (**P**)

- **Repeated reading strategies** have **helped** _____ gain **confidence** in reading as his/her **reading fluency increases** with each lesson. He/she has **learned how to study the pattern** and **make-up** of **individual words that** he/she **finds difficult to read**. (**P**)

- _____ **reads regularly** and **always volunteers to read aloud** to his/her classmates. **Repeated reading** exercises, regular **study of words, word patterns**, and **teacher assisted reading** are **helping** _____ make **tangible progress** in reading **fluency**. _____ is encouraged to **read daily** in order to maintain this progress. (**P**)

Positive/Negative

- _____ often **volunteers to read aloud** in class and this has helped him/her improve **fluency, decoding,** and **reading comprehension** skills. _____ is encouraged to **select meaningful reading material** (*such as illustrated novels/ magazines/ comics/ newspapers*) and **read regularly at home** and at school. **Daily reading** at home, and the filling out of the biweekly **Home Reading Log**, must be done as instructed. (**P,N**)

- _____ **struggles through reading** of books, but demonstrates a **good understanding** of **content** and **perspective**. (**N,P**)

- _____ **reads with difficulty**, but his/her **enthusiasm** and **eagerness to improve continue**. He/she **struggles to recognize** many **commonly used words** and **rarely identifies** and **decodes unfamiliar words**. **Main idea** and **order of information** are accurately **comprehended** (understood) some of the time. (**N,P**)

- In spite of always volunteering to read aloud to classmates, **reading fluency continues** to be an area that **requires attention**. **Repeated reading** exercises, regular **study of words, word patterns,** and **teacher assisted reading** have been very helpful in improving reading fluency. _____ is encouraged to read daily (aloud if possible) in order to maintain this progress. (**N,P**)

Negative

- A **larger sight vocabulary would contribute** to _____'s improved fluency and reading comprehension. (**N**)

- _____ continues to **decode unfamiliar words** through the use of strategies **with some success** and assistance. Daily, **regular reading** at home (throughout the school year) **is highly recommended,** as it will help _____ maintain and improve reading skills. (**N**)

- **Volunteering to read in class** and **reading daily** at home **highly recommended** for _____ in order to increase familiarity with and exposure to new words. Continual **exposure** to **written words increases** the **repertoire of decoding strategies** and improves **reading comprehension**. The biweekly **Home Reading Log** must be completed as instructed. (**N**)

- _____ is **starting to demonstrate** (*some/ more/ much*) **confidence** in his/her reading. With encouragement _____ **attempts** to **read independently** and **aloud during class**. _____ needs to **decode** words more consistently, remembering to apply the **strategies** learned in class. (**N**)

Attitude Toward Reading

Positive

- _____ **has responded well** to **our reading program** that encourages the reading of different **high-interest materials**, **daily reading**, learning of **reading comprehension strategies**, and authentic and **relevant reading experiences**. _____ **enjoys reading** in class and **makes good use** of **reading opportunities**. (**P,P**)

- _____ **continues to volunteer to read aloud** during class. He/she **has started to incorporate the** discussed **reading strategies** (*i.e., pausing at punctuation*) to become a more fluent reader. _____ is **encouraged to access** and use any **reading material** of interest **available** in our **classroom and** the **library**, and also read (every night/ regularly/ daily) for pleasure. (**P**)

Negative

- It is **recommended** that _____ **carry to class reading material** in which he/she has an interest. To this point, _____ has **not shown** an **interest in reading any of the books** available for reading in our class or the **school library**. (**N**)

Oral Communication

General

- _____'s **communicates** (shares/expresses) **ideas**, **opinions,** thoughts, and feelings with (*little/ some/ much*) **clarity** and **confidence**. (**G**)

- _____'s **ideas** and **opinions** (thoughts and feelings) are **communicated** with (*little/ some/ much*) clarity and **coherence** (**G**)

- _____'s (*language/ some language/ most language*) used in **presentations** is **hard to follow** and **understand**. (**G**)

- _____'s **conveys ideas** with (*little/ some/ much*) **coherence** and (*little/ some/much*) **accuracy** for different (simple) **purposes**. (**G**)

- _____'s (*with reminders and teacher supervision/ most of the time/ consistently* and *willingly*) **listens to discussions** on familiar topics and **asks relevant questions**. (**G**)

- _____'s (*rarely/ sometimes/ often*) uses **eye contact**, **variations in pace**, and appropriate **gestures** in oral presentations. (**G**)

- _____'s (*rarely/ frequently/ most of the time/ consistently/ always*) **participates** in class and shows (*limited/ some good/ excellent*) **ability to concentrate** and **stay on topic**. (**G**)

- _____'s (*rarely/ sometimes/ usually/ consistently*) **contributes** to class by expressing ideas and opinions and **volunteering answers** to questions. (**G**)

- _____'s **ideas** and **opinions are shared** (*without much coherence and in limited ways/ with some coherence and accuracy/ clearly and accurately for distinct purposes/ clearly, accurately, and confidently for different purposes and in a wide range of contexts*). (**G**)

Positive

- _____ continues to show **steady gains**. (**P**)

- _____ **stays on topic during** class **discussions**. (**P**)

- _____ **responds** to **questions** and **inquiries effectively**. (**P**)

- _____ **asks insightful, relevant,** and **appropriate questions**. (**P**)

- _____'s **verbal communication skills** (continue to) show **steady gains**. (**P**)

- _____ has **participated** in class **oral presentations** with **much success**. (**P**)

- _____'s **verbal communication skills** are showing **steady** and **consistent improvement**. (**P**)

- _____ **listens** and **responds thoughtfully** to **different ideas** and **viewpoints**. (**P**)

- _____ **retells** personal **experiences** and events **with passion**, **enthusiasm**, and **clarity**. (**P**)

- _____ **has the ability to hold focused discussions** (with peers with others) related to school work. (**P**)

- _____ **volunteers regularly** "additional" **information** in response to specific questions. (**P**)

- _____'s **language used** in **presentations** is **well chosen**, **easy to follow**, and easy to **understand**. (**P**)

- _____ **participates often** in **class** and is **willing to answer questions** and **offer suggestions**. (**P**)

- _____ **speaks clearly**, using **appropriate tone of voice** when making **presentations**. (**P**)

- _____ **participates regularly** in class discussions and **volunteers personal opinions** (**P**)

- _____ is an **enthusiastic learner** who **enjoys group activities** and **socializing** with his/her peers. (**P**)

- _____ **uses** and **selects appropriate words during conversations** and **when asking questions**. (**P**)

- _____ **confidently uses appropriate tone of voice** and **gestures** in social and classroom activities. (**P**)

- _____ **responds effectively**, **appropriately**, and **clearly to** specific **questions**, **ideas**, and **opinions**. (**P**)

- _____ **participates in group discussions**, **using appropriate language** and **complete sentences**. (**P**)

- _____ **expresses** his/her **ideas** and **opinions confidently**, but **without trying to dominate discussions**. (**P**)

- _____ **asks** and **answers questions** thoughtfully on a wide range of topics **to get** and **clarify information**. (**P**)

- _____ **listens** and (*rarely/ does not interrupt/ sometimes interrupts*) the class **with off-the-topic comments**. (**P**)

Report Card and IEP Comments

- _____ **shows an ability to pay attention** in class, **asking** and **appropriately answering** relevant **questions**. (**P**)

- _____ **participates often** in class and **shows ability to concentrate** by **identifying** the **main points** and **staying on topic**. (**P**)

- **Some progress was observed**, and _____ is to be commended for his/her **willingness** and **enthusiasm to succeed**. (**P**)

- _____ **volunteers more frequently** to **give answers** and **contribute to classroom discussions** in front of his/her classmates. (**P**)

- _____ **listens** to others **without interrupting** and (is encouraged to) actively **participate(s)** in all class **discussions** and group activities. (**P**)

- _____ **has participated more actively** in class activities (and discussions) this term and **become a more confident communicator** (speaker). (**P**)

- _____ **consistently listens** and **respects opinions of others**. _____ **communicates effectively** and **contributes information** to the class and group members. (**P**)

- With encouragement, _____ **is beginning to interact with** his/her **peers** during unstructured learning times. He/she **is beginning to contribute** his/her **ideas in a small class setting** (without impulsive/regular disruptions). (**P**)

- _____ **participated enthusiastically in** (*all/ most/ majority of*) **oral presentations. Speaking more slowly**, and **planning ahead** by **preparing** an **outline**, **would ensure better understanding** of the spoken message **by listeners**. (**P**)

- _____ has **participated more actively** in class activities and discussions this term and **become a** (much more) **confident speaker**. He/she, likewise, **volunteers more often to answer questions and contribute to classroom discussions** in front of other classmates. (**P**)

- With encouragement, _____ is **beginning to interact with** his/her **peers** during unstructured learning oppurtunity. _____ **is beginning to contribute** his/her **ideas** in a small class setting, without interruptions. _____ **is becoming more self-confident** in **social situations**, both in class and elsewhere in the school. (**P**)

Positive/Negative

- _____ **continues to improve** in this area, **but** at a **slower pace**. (Impulsive) **verbal interruptions** (outbursts) and **negativity** by _____ are **hindering learning**. (**P,N**)

- _____ has **enjoyed presenting in front of the class** and (*always/ often*) **volunteers** to be the **first** to **perform**/do **assigned tasks. Forming long sentences** and **presenting ideas** in an **order** that **makes sense** is **still an area** with room **for improvement**. (**P,N**)

- _____ **participates often in** class, willingly **answering questions** and **offering suggestions**; however, **limited ability** to **concentrate** and **stay on topic make clear communication difficult**. _____ is **encouraged** to **make** a **conscious effort** to **speak** at a **slower** pace, focusing on **clear** and **accurate enunciation** of words. **(P,N)**

- _____ **participates eagerly** in **group discussions, but** has **difficulty with knowing when to talk, when to listen,** and **how much to say**. **(P,N,N)**

- _____ **volunteers often** to **answer questions** during class discussions; **however, frequent distractibility** is at times (often/usually) a **hindrance** to **successful** and **appropriate communication** with teachers and peers. **(P,N,N)**

- **Although** _____ **still needs** to learn to **project** his/her **voice** when speaking, his/her ability to communicate **has clearly** (definitely) **improved**. **(N,P)**

Negative

- _____'s **speech** continues to be **presented in short phrases** or **single words**. **(N)**

- Verbal communication is **inaudible, unclear,** and **difficult to understand**. **(N,** quiet)

- _____ **enunciates** words **quickly** and is **often difficult to understand**. **(N)**

- _____ has **difficulty expressing ideas** in a **clear** and **concise manner**. **(N)**

- _____ is encouraged to **contribute** information and **ideas** more often. **(N,** quiet)

- _____ **needs to listen to others** and **work more cooperatively** in a group. **(N)**

- _____ is **encouraged to volunteer answers** and **participate** orally (more often). **(N,** quiet)

- Verbal **communication is improving**, but **still inaudible** and **difficult to understand**. **(N,** quiet)

- _____ is encouraged to **volunteer and express** his/her **opinion** in class **more often**. **(N,** quiet)

- _____'s **interrupting the lesson** or **other speakers** takes away from the flow of classroom activities. **(N)**

- _____ **requires urging** to **use verbal expression** and **engage** in **class discussions**. **(N)**

- _____ **must learn** to **respect opinions** of others and **take responsibility for his/her own actions**. **(N)**

- Oral communication is **still an area of struggle** for _____ and **will continue** to **need attention**. (**N**)

- _____ **continues to experience difficulty expressing ideas** in a clear and concise manner. (**N**)

- _____'s **forming sentences** and **presenting ideas** in a **logical order** are still areas with room for improvement. (**N**)

- _____ has a **limited sense** of **when to end verbal communication** with his/her teachers and peers. (**N**)

- _____ is **encouraged to remain focused** during class and **restrict comments** to **lesson-related topics**. (**N**)

- _____ **sometimes gets involved** in class **discussions** and **shares** his/her opinion, knowledge, and views. (**N**)

- _____ **continues** to **require urging** to use **verbal expression** and engage in class discussions more frequently. (**N**)

- _____ **participates eagerly** in discussions, **but** often **needs reminders** to **settle down** and **focus** on the relevant topic. (**N**)

- _____ is **encouraged to participate more frequently** in class discussions and **ask questions** in order **to clarify** his/her **thinking**. (**N**)

- _____ is **encouraged to resist** the **temptation** to **vocalize displeasure** to the **entire class** when things don't turn out as expected. (**N**)

- _____ **engaged in noticeably fewer oral discussions** and was **less willing** (unwilling) to express/share ideas and opinions this term. (**N**)

- _____ is **encouraged** to **become a more focused listener, giving others** a **chance** to **fully express their opinion** before interrupting. (**N**)

- Despite **enthusiastic participation** in class, _____ **often speaks out of impulse, with** a **limited sense of when to speak,** and **for how long**. (**N**)

- _____ is **encouraged to participate in class** and **group activities** and **ask questions to clarify meaning** and **ensure understanding**. (**N**)

- _____ sometimes **experiences** a noticeable **lack of confidence** when faced with having **to formally express** himself/herself through an **oral presentation**. (**N**)

- _____ **sometimes gets involved** in class **discussions** and **shares** his/her opinion, knowledge, and views. He/she is **encouraged to volunteer answers** and **participate** orally more often. (**N**)

- _____ **continues to require urging** to **use verbal expression** and engage in class discussions more often. **Greater participation** leads to improved ability to use successful **verbal expression** in **group** situations. (**N**)

- _____ **requires urging** and **prompting to use verbal expression** and **engage in class discussions**. He/she is encouraged to strive toward becoming a more confident and skilled speaker by **taking part** more often in **class discussions**. (**N**)

- _____ still **requires urging to use verbal expression** and **engage in class discussions**. He/she is **encouraged to strive** toward being a more confident and skilled speaker by participating more often in **class discussions**. (**N**)

- _____ sometimes **experiences** a **lack of confidence** when faced with having **to formally express** himself/herself through **oral presentations**. He/she is **encouraged to be** completely/well **prepared**, and **rehearsed** when faced with having to present in front of others. This will help increase his/her level of **confidence** and reduce **anxiety**. (**N**)

- _____ **participates eagerly** in group discussions **but has difficulty with knowing when to talk, when to listen**, and **how much to say**. (**P,N,N**)

- _____ **has a limited sense** of **when to end verbal communication** with teachers and peers. (**N,N**)

- **Distractibility often prevents successful** and **appropriate communication** with teacher and peers. (**N,N**)

- **Demonstrating** a sense of **when to speak, when to listen**, and **how much to say remains** a **challenge** for_____. (**N,N**)

- _____ **often appears to be speaking out of impulse, with a limited sense of when to speak** and **for how long**. (**N,N**)

- Oral communication **continues to be an area of struggle** and **will require continued assistance**. Many of _____'s **spoken sentences** are **broken**, and often voiced using **incorrect** (wrong) **verb tense**. (**N,N**)

- _____ is **easily distracted**. He/she **needs constant encouragement to stay focused** on the task at hand. _____ is reminded that he/she **must concentrate on** his/her **own work** and progress without being **distracted** by other activities around him/her. (**N,N,N**)

- _____ often seems to be **speaking out of impulse, with** a **limited sense of when to speak** and **for how long. Frequent distractibility** and **lack of focus** (are a **major concern**/ have often **hindered** successful communication with teachers and peers). (**N,N,N**)

Report Card and IEP Comments

Articulation and Intelligible Speech

General

- _____ **has shown** (*little/ some/ good*) **progress** in the area of articulation/intelligible speech. (**G**)

- _____ (*rarely/ sometimes/ usually/ always*) **listens to the instructions** given in class by the teacher and asks relevant questions. (**G**)

Positive

- **Some progress was observed**, and _____ is to **be commended** for his/her **willingness and enthusiasm to succeed**. (**P**)

- _____ **works** (*daily/ weekly/ regularly*) **with a speech and language pathologist**. In class, he/she **puts forth a good effort** to practice **pronunciation** of words. (**P**)

- Working on **word wheels**, studying **spelling patterns**, providing a **supportive reading environment**, and **reading regularly** (repeated reading) **are helping** _____ with speech articulation difficulties. (**P**)

Positive/Negative

- _____ **is making an effort** and **improving at making** his/her **speech and word articulation more intelligible**. _____ **has become more talkative** and has been observed **asking questions** on a more regular basis. **Spoken words are still difficult to hear**, and **somewhat inaudible**. _____ is **encouraged to continue to take chances and speak using a louder voice** during conversation/communication with others. (**P,N**)

Negative

- _____ **continues to slur** his/her **words** and **struggle** with **word articulation**. (**N**)

- **Very little progress** in articulation and intelligible speech has been made **in spite of** _____'s **many** applied/attempted **strategies**. (**N**)

- _____ **must practice speaking at a slower pace** so that the spoken words can be understood by others. (**N**)

- **Distractibility** often (frequently) **prevents** _____'s **successful and appropriate communication** with teachers and peers. (**N**)

Copyright © 2001, 2003, 2009 by Stevan Krajnjan

- _____ **requires teacher support and assistance** to help him/her **with enunciation** of words and speech **clarity**. (**N**)

- **Very little progress** in **articulation** and **intelligible speech** has been made in spite of application of different strategies. _____ **requires teacher support and assistance** to help him/her **with enunciation** of words and **clarity** of speech. (**N**)

- Making an **effort to project** his/her **voice** when speaking **would help** _____ **improve articulation** and **speech difficulties**. _____ **needs frequent reminders to speak with a louder voice** in order for the spoken words to be heard and understood. (**N**)

- **Very little progress** in articulation and intelligible speech has been made **in spite of** the many applied **strategies**. _____ **continues to slur** his/her **words** and **struggle** with **word articulation. Reading aloud** on a regular basis and **speaking at a slower rate is encouraged**. (**N**)

- _____ **continues to struggle with making** his/her **speech and word articulation more intelligible. To compensate** for this, _____ **often withdraws, keeps to himself/herself**, and **remains silent and uninvolved. Spoken words are usually inaudible, broken,** and **difficult to hear**. (**N**)

- Working on **word wheels**, studying **spelling patterns**, providing a **supportive reading environment**, and **reading regularly** (repeated reading) **are helping** _____ with speech articulation difficulties. To make further gains, _____ is encouraged to **continue to read aloud** at a **slow pace**, focusing on **clarity** of word **enunciation. Adult supervision** and **assistance would help** with this task. (**N**)

- Working on **word wheels** (**consonant blends**), studying **spelling patterns**, providing a **supportive reading environment**, and **reading regularly** (repeated reading) are **making a small difference** in _____'s ability to articulate words. To make further gains, _____ needs to **continue to read aloud** at a slow pace, **focusing on clarity** of word **enunciation**. In addition, _____ **must practice speaking at a slower pace** so that the spoken words can be understood by others. (**N**)

- _____ often appears to be **speaking out of impulse, with a** (very) **limited sense of when to speak and for how long. Frequent distractibility** and lack of focus (are **major concerns/ have often hindered** successful communication with teachers and peers). (**N,N**)

- _____ **continues to struggle with making** his/her **speech and word articulation more intelligible. To compensate** for this, _____ **often withdraws, keeps to himself/herself**, and **remains silent** and **uninvolved. Spoken words are usually inaudible, broken,** and **difficult to hear**. _____ is **encouraged to take chances** and **speak** using a **louder voice** when communicating with others. (**N,N**)

Listening Skills

General

- _____ (*rarely/ sometimes/ usually/ always*) **listens to the instructions** given in class by the teacher and asks relevant questions. (**G**)

Positive

- _____ **listens to ideas of others**. (**P**)

- _____ is an **improved** and **more patient listener**. (**P**)

- _____ **consistently listens** and **respects the opinions of others**. (**P**)

- _____ is **getting better at listening to opinions** and **ideas of others**. (**P**)

- _____ **listens** and **does not interrupt** the class **with off-the-topic comments**. (**P**)

- _____ **consistently listens to, acknowledges,** and **considers differing opinions** of his/her classmates. (**P**)

- **Some progress was observed**, and _____ is to be commended for his/her **willingness and enthusiasm to succeed**. (**P**)

- During this term, _____ **made** regular **contributions** to classroom discussions, **consciously wording opinions** in a **less critical manner**. (**P**)

- _____ is **getting better at listening to opinions** and **ideas of others**. _____ also **knows when it is appropriate to interrupt** and **for how long to speak**. (**P**)

- _____ **appears to be listening to** the **instructions** as they are given. He/she is **encouraged to rephrase** the **directions back to the teacher**, in order **to ensure complete understanding**. (**P**)

- _____ is an **improved** and **more patient listener**. He/she has made **good progress** in giving other speakers a chance to fully express their opinion prior to **offering a personal opinion**. During this term, _____ **made** regular **contributions** to classroom discussions, **consciously wording opinions** in a **less critical manner**. (**P**)

Report Card and IEP Comments

Positive/Negative

- _____ **continues to improve** in this area **but at a slower pace. Verbal interruptions** and **negativity** by _____ are **hindering learning. (P,N)**

- _____ has shown **some progress** in the area of listening skills. He/she **sometimes requires reminders to listen** to the opinions and ideas of others as well, **especially in small group discussions**, where everyone deserves a chance to be heard. **(P,N)**

- _____ has shown **some progress** in the area of listening skills. He/she still **requires frequent reminders to pay attention** during class time. _____ is **listening to** the **ideas** of others with some teacher supervision. **(N,P)**

Negative

- **Better concentration** in class **would improve** _____'s **achievement** in this and other areas. **(N)**

- _____ still **requires frequent reminders to pay attention during class time. (N)**

- Listening skills and **following directions** continue to **pose challenges** for _____. **(N)**

- _____ **needs to focus more on teacher's directions** and **less on** his/her **peers. (N)**

- _____'s **interrupting the lesson** or other speakers **takes away from the flow** of classroom activities. **(N)**

- _____'s **criticizing** of other individuals' **opinions** needs to be **worded in a gentler and nonthreatening way. (N)**

- _____ is **encouraged to listen patiently to** the **opinions of others** and **wait for** his/her **turn to speak. (N)**

- **Distractibility** often (frequently) prevents _____'s successful and appropriate communication with teachers and peers. **(N)**

- _____ is **encouraged to listen and consider ideas of others, without interrupting** and being **negative. (N)**

- Despite sitting at the front and close to the teacher, _____ **still finds it difficult to follow directions or initiate tasks. (N)**

- _____ is **encouraged to resist the temptation to vocalize displeasure to the entire class** when things don't turn out as expected. (**N**)

- In order for _____ to listen well, he/she (*sometimes/ often/ usually*) **needs reminders to clear** his/her **desk,** and to **make** some **eye contact** with the teacher (*speaker*). **Rephrasing instructions** to _____ helps to ensure his/her understanding. (**N**)

- Listening skills and **following directions** continue to **pose challenges** for _____. Despite selective (strategic) seating, _____ **still finds it difficult to follow directions or initiate tasks**. He/she **needs to focus more on teacher's directions** and **less on activities of** his/her **peers**. (**N**)

- _____ is **encouraged to listen patiently to** the **opinions of others** and **wait for** his/her **turn to speak. Interrupting** the **lesson** or **other speakers** takes away from the flow of classroom activities. _____'s **criticizing** of other individuals' **opinions** needs to be **worded** in a **gentler** and **nonthreatening way**. (**N**)

- **Demonstrating** a **sense of when to speak, when to listen,** and **how much to say remains a challenge** for _____. (**N,N**)

- _____ often **speaks out of impulse, with a limited sense of when to speak and for how long. Frequent distractibility** and lack of focus (are **major concerns**) **have often hindered** successful communication with teachers and peers. (**N,N**)

Homework Completion

General

- Assignments are **completed by due dates** and (*sometimes/ usually/ always/ consistently*) **display care** and effort. (**G**)

General/Negative

- _____ has (*sometimes/ often*) **neglected to submit assignments** by due date. (**G,N**)

Positive

- _____ **completes** homework **on time** and **with care**. (**P**)

- **Assignments** are completed **with care** and **effort** by due dates. (**P**)

- It is noted that **homework completion** was **more consistent** this term. (**P**)

- _____ always **completes homework with effort** and **diligence**. (**P**)

- _____ often **completes** his/her homework **on time** and with care. (**P**)

- _____ **puts forth a consistent effort** to complete homework on time. (**P**)

- _____ **consistently completes** assignments **on time** and **with care**. (**P**)

- _____ **accepts responsibility** for completing tasks on time and with care. (**P**)

- _____ **consistently finishes** homework assignments on time and with care. (**P**)

- Assignments are **completed** by due dates, usually with **satisfactory care** and **effort**. (**P**)

- **Majority** of assignments are completed by due dates with satisfactory care and effort. (**P**)

- _____ **consistently completes** and submits all assignments for evaluation **on time**. (**P**)

- _____ **completes** assignments by due dates, but **not always to the best of** his/her **ability**. (**P**)

- _____ **consistently completes** assignments on time and with care. He/she **works well** without supervision, as he/she **is able to follow routines** and instructions independently. (**P**)

- _____ uses his/her **planner** with **little direction** from the teacher and usually **completes homework on time**. (**P**)

- **Some progress was observed**, and _____ is **to be commended** for his/her **willingness and enthusiasm to succeed**. (**P**)

- _____ **uses** his/her **planner/organizer with little direction** from the teacher and **completes** homework **on time** and **with care**. (**P**)

- It is noted that **homework completion** was **more consistent** this term. _____ has also made noticeable effort to **improve the quality of work** done in class. (**P**)

- **With** teacher **assistance**, _____ **is learning to use** his/her school **organizer to** help him/her **record important events, reminders, tests**, and **homework assignments** that need to be completed. (**P**)

Positive/Negative

- Assignments are **completed by due dates** and, while there has been some evidence of greater care and effort, _____'s **commitment to high-quality work must continue to improve**. (**P,N**)

- _____ has made **some effort in completing homework**, assigned **tasks,** and **returning classroom materials**. A **more consistent and independent use** of our **school organizer** is **highly recommended**. (**P,N**)

- _____ is a **very considerate student** who continues to have some **difficulty** completing **assignments** on time. (**P,N**)

- _____ **needs to forge ahead and strive** to complete all homework assignments on time; however, he/she is to be **commended for** the tremendous (awesome/ exceptional/ incredible) **increase in effort** on tasks performed in class. (**N,P**)

- **Inconsistent homework completion** remains a **serious concern** and a **hindrance** to learning. _____ **needs to assume greater responsibility** for establishing and maintaining an effective study/homework routine next year. An **increase in effort** on in-class tasks was **observed** in the latter part of the third term. (**N,P**)

Negative

- All homework must be **completed on time**. (**N**)

- **Regular completion** of assigned homework **is required**. (**N**)

- _____ often **arrives** to class **without** his/her **homework**. (**N**)

- **Incomplete homework** and **lack of effort** are hindering progress. (**N**)

- **Regular neglect of homework** assignments has had an effect on progress. (**N**)

Copyright © 2001, 2003, 2009 by Stevan Krajnjan

- Several _____ homework assignments **have not been completed**. **(N)**

- _____ **must ensure** that all **homework** tasks are **completed on time**. **(N)**

- To **progress** academically, homework completion is an area that **must improve**. **(N)**

- **Inconsistent completion** of homework is a **concern**, especially in _____. **(N)**

- _____ **needs to continue to strive to complete** all homework assignments. **(N)**

- **Assignments** are **often incomplete**, **submitted late** for marking, or **not handed in** at all. **(N)**

- Many **homework assignments** have **not** been **completed** and submitted for evaluation. **(N)**

- **Homework** assignments are **not always completed on time** and to the best of ability. **(N)**

- _____ **completes** his/her homework on time, **although not always with care**. **(N)**

- _____ needs to ensure that all **assigned work** is **completed** and **handed in on time**. **(N)**

- Assignments **are completed** by due dates, **but don't** always **display** proper **care** and **effort**. **(N)**

- **Inconsistent homework completion** remains a (serious) **concern** and a hindrance to learning. **(N)**

- **Adequate** and **regular completion** of homework **remains an area that needs to improve**. **(N)**

- _____ needs to show more **initiative** when working on **assignments**, and avoid **distractions**. **(N)**

- _____ has experienced **some difficulty** in meeting due dates and completing assignments. **(N)**

- **Completion** of homework is **inconsistent** and often **not done according to instructions**. **(N)**

- _____ **requires** constant **reminders to finish** his/her **work and hand in assignments**. **(N)**

- **Greater degree of voluntary class participation is encouraged**. All **homework** must also be completed. **(N)**

- _____ **must accept responsibility** for **recording homework** and **completing assigned tasks on time**. **(N)**

- Many (numerous/ most) **homework** and **class assignments** are **not completed** and **submitted** for evaluation. **(N)**

Report Card and IEP Comments

- School **organizer needs to be used independently** and **as instructed**, and all **homework completed on time**. (**N**)

- _____ **inconsistently completes** homework assignments and **requires reminders** to work independently. (**N**)

- **Despite ample class time** and **remedial** opportunities, **some homework** and **long-term** assigned work remain **unfinished**. (**N**)

- All homework **must be completed on time**. **Lack of homework completion** has had an **effect on the** (overall, final) **mark** (this term). (**N**)

- A **more effective use** of his/her school **planner/organizer should help** _____ keep track of assignments and due dates. (**N**)

- . . . **however,** he/she **needs to improve** his/her **level of commitment** and **concentration** on daily tasks and on **long-term assignments**. (**N**)

- _____ is (strongly/ very much) **encouraged** to establish a daily **homework** routine that ensures **completion** of all assigned work. (**N**)

- Taking the school **planner/organizer** home and **setting aside** regular **time for homework** is a routine that **must be adhered to** on a daily basis. (**N**)

- _____ has **not completed** or **submitted** required work in _____ despite generous **class time** and **remedial opportunities**. (**N**)

- _____ has **not completed** the required work in _____ **despite ample** class **time** and **remedial opportunities**. (**N**)

- _____ is **encouraged to take** his/her **organizer home** each day and **set aside regular time for completion** of **homework** assignments. (**N**)

- _____ has made **limited progress in areas of organizational skills, homework completion, social skills,** and **interpersonal relationships**. (**N**)

- It is recommended that _____ **complete all homework to the best of ability** and **seek teacher assistance** when **concepts** are not understood. (**N**)

- **In spite** of **daily assistance** and frequent **reminders,** many homework and class assignments were **not completed** and **submitted** for evaluation. (**N**)

- **Greater consistency in homework completion,** improved **study habits,** and regular **participation in class** would help improve academic achievement. (**N**)

- **Assignments** are **often incomplete, submitted late** for marking, or **not handed in at all.** _____ is **encouraged to work more independently** in class. (**N**)

- _____ **must accept responsibility for recording homework** and long-term **assignments** in his/her **organizer** and for **completing tasks on time**. (**N**)

- _____ **must accept responsibility** for **recording homework** and for **completing assigned tasks on time**, and **rely less on others** to do this for him/her. (**N**)

- **In spite of** the **learning strategies** that are in place, _____ **does not complete** and **submit** for marking (*many/ most/ all*) of his/her assignments on time. (**N**)

- _____ **needs to improve** his/her level of **commitment** and **concentration** on daily tasks and on **completion of homework** and long-term assignments. (**N**)

- _____ is **encouraged** to take his **planner/organizer** home each day and **set aside regular time** for completion of **homework** assignments and **reading**. (**N**)

- _____ **needs to** improve his/her **level of commitment** and **concentration on daily tasks** and on **completion of homework** and **long-term assignments**. (**N**)

- **Timely completion** of **homework** and **daily recording** of homework in the **planner/organizer must be in place** if _____'s learning is to continue to improve. (**N**)

- _____ **needs to assume greater responsibility** for establishing and maintaining effective use of **planner/organizer**, **study**, and **homework** completion **routines**. (**N**)

- _____ needs to assume **greater responsibility** for **maintenance and effective use of school organizer**, and **development of a consistent homework routine**. (**N**)

- It is **recommended** that _____ (*sets/establishes*) a daily **homework routine** that would help/ensure **adequate completion of all assigned work** and improve chances of academic success. (**N**)

- **Timely completion** of **homework**, **studying for tests**, and daily independent **recording of homework** in the **organizer** must be in place if _____'s academic achievement is to continue to improve. (**N**)

- _____ needs to ensure that all **assigned work** is completed and **handed in on time**. **Greater degree of focus** in class and **more consistent work habits** would help improve academic achievement. (**N**)

- It is (again) **recommended** that _____ **assume greater responsibility** for maintenance and **effective use of** school **planner/organizer**, and development of a **consistent homework routine**. (**N**)

- _____ uses his/her **organizer** to record important events, dates, and information; **however**, he/she **needs to improve** his/her level of **commitment** and **concentration** on daily tasks and on **completion of homework** and long-term assignments. (**N**)

- _____ is generally a **very considerate student** who continues to have some **difficulty** completing **assignments** on time. **Establishing a consistent study** and **homework routine** must become one of _____'s (*second/ third*) term **goals**. (**N**)

Report Card and IEP Comments

- _____ must ensure that all **homework** tasks are completed on time. It is **recommended** that _____ **assume greater responsibility** for maintenance and effective use of his/her school **planner/organizer,** and development of a **consistent homework routine**. (**N**)

- _____ must learn to use the **planner/organizer** as a practical tool that reminds him/her of **homework**, due dates, and other important information. _____ is **strongly encouraged** to establish a daily **homework** routine that ensures completion of all assigned work. (**N**)

- **Despite ample class time** and **remedial opportunities**, some **homework** and long-term assigned work **remains unfinished**. Timely **completion of homework** and **daily recording** of it in the **planner/organizer** must be in place if _____'s learning is to continue to (*improve/ experience success in academic subjects*). (**N**)

- _____ uses his/her **organizer** to record daily classroom activities and **homework** assignments, but **often neglects to complete** and **bring** them to school **on time**. It is **recommended** that _____ set/establish a daily **homework routine** that would help/ensure adequate completion of all assigned work and improve chances of academic success. (**N**)

- **Homework completion** and appropriate use of the **planner/organizer**, however, **remain a concern**. _____ is encouraged to take his/her **planner/organizer** home each day and **set aside regular time** for completion of **homework** assignments and reading. All **classroom equipment** must be ready for use and brought to class in working condition on daily basis. (**N**)

- Many **homework assignments** have **not** been **completed** and **submitted** for evaluation. If _____ is to make further academic gains, this is an area that needs to improve. (**N,N**)

- Numerous **homework assignments** have **not** been **completed** and **submitted** for evaluation. **This is a very serious issue that needs to be addressed** in the future if _____ is to make any further academic gains. (**N,N**)

- **In spite** of **daily assistance** and frequent **reminders**, many homework and class assignments were **not completed** and **submitted** for evaluation. For to progress academically this is an area that must improve. (**N,N**)

- **Despite flexible due dates**, opportunities for **remediation, encouragement** and **reminders** to use the **school agenda, many homework** and class assignments **were not completed** and **submitted** for evaluation. (**N,N**)

- _____ often **arrives** to class **without** his/her **homework**. He/she **requires** regular **reminders to finish work and hand in assignments**. _____ needs to use the school **planner/organizer** on a daily basis to monitor the work he/she has to complete. (**N,N,N**)

Next Steps

- _____ is **encouraged to hand in** all **assignments** by the due date. (**NS**)

- _____ is **encouraged to use** his/her **organizer** and complete all homework tasks **daily**. (**NS**)

- _____ is **encouraged to** seek (_remedial help/ teacher assistance_) **when concepts are unclear** or difficult. (**NS**)

- _____ is **encouraged to** show more attention to **care** and **detail in class work and assignments**. (**NS**)

- _____ is **encouraged to complete** (continue completing) his/her homework **on time** and with care. (**NS**)

- _____ is **encouraged to** demonstrate responsibility in **attitude, attendance, punctuality,** and **task completion**. (**NS**)

- _____ is **encouraged to complete** tasks (assignments/ homework) consistently, **on time,** and **with care**. (**NS**)

- _____ is **encouraged to** put forth a **consistent effort** in completing his/her assignments on time and with care. (**NS**)

- _____ is **encouraged** to work on improving the **neatness** of **written work, consistently, in all subjects,** and **submit it on time**. (**NS**)

Report Card and IEP Comments

Use of Student Planner/Organizer

Throughout the following comments, the word "organizer" is used in place of other similar words and phrases, such as "school agenda," "school planner," "student planner," and "student organizer." Select the words that best suit your reporting needs.

General

- School organizer is (*rarely/ sometimes/ usually/ always*) **used as instructed**. (**G**)

- _____ **uses** his/her planner **with** (*much/ some/ little*) direction from the teacher. (**G**)

- _____ **makes** (*poor/ satisfactory/ good*) **use** of his/her organizer **for long-term planning**. (**G**)

- School organizer is **used as instructed** (*with/ only with/ with some/ with little/ without*) teacher supervision. (**G**)

- _____ **continues to make** (*good/ very good/ effective/ very effective/ excellent*) **use** of his/her organizer. (**G**)

- _____ (*sometimes/ often/ usually/ always*) **uses** his/her organizer to record important information and dates. (**G**)

- _____ (*rarely/ sometimes/ usually/ always*) **uses** his/her organizer to **record important dates** and **information**. (**G**)

- School organizer (*needs to be/ must be/ is/ is always*) used **independently** and **as instructed** (and all homework is completed on time). (**G**)

Positive

- _____ continues to use his/her organizer **well**. (**P**)

- School organizer is **used consistently** and **as instructed**. (**P**)

- _____ **demonstrates effective use** of his/her organizer. (**P**)

- _____ **continues to make good use** of his/her organizer. (**P**)

- _____ has regularly **kept the organizer complete** and **up-to-date**. (**P**)

- _____ uses his/her school organizer **consistently** and as instructed. (**P**)

- _____ is **encouraged to continue** using his/her organizer **effectively**. (**P**)

- _____ makes **effective use** of his/her school organizer. (**P**)

- _____ continues to use his/her organizer in a **satisfactory** manner. (**P**)

- _____ **uses** his/her school organizer **consistently** and as instructed. (**P**)

- Using his/her organizer daily has been an **excellent** tool for work completion. (**P**)

- _____ (often) uses his/her organizer **to record important information, events,** and dates. (**P**)

- **Using** his/her **organizer** to **record assignments** and to **communicate with home has been beneficial**. (**P**)

- _____ makes **satisfactory** use of his/her organizer, but is **not as effective** as the (*first/ second*) term. (**P**)

- _____ **effectively** and **consistently records** all the **required information** in his/her school **organizer**. (**P**)

- _____ **uses** his/her planner **with little direction** from the teacher and **completes homework on time** and with care. (**P**)

- _____ uses his/her planner **with little direction** from the teacher and usually **completes** his/her **homework on time**. (**P**)

- _____ demonstrates **effective use of** his/her **organizer,** and his/her **work consistently** exhibits **thought** and **care**. (**P**)

- **Some progress was observed**, and _____ is **to be commended** for his/her **willingness and enthusiasm to succeed**. (**P**)

- **Timely completion of homework, studying for tests, and daily independent recording** of homework in the organizer **must be in place** if _____'s academic achievement is to continue to improve. (**P**)

Positive/Negative

- _____ uses **organizer** to record daily classroom activities and homework assignments but often **neglects to complete** and **bring them to school** on time. (**P,N**)

- _____ has made **some effort to complete assigned homework** and **tasks** and **return materials**. A **more consistent and independent use** of the **school organizer** is **highly recommended**. (**P,N**)

- _____ uses his/her **organizer to record important events**, **dates,** and **information;** however, he/she **needs to** improve his/her **level of commitment** and **concentration on daily tasks** and **completion of homework** and long-term assignments. (**P,N**)

- _____ uses his/her **organizer** to record daily classroom activities and homework assignments, but often **neglects to complete** and **bring them to school** on time. It is **recommended** that _____ **establish a daily homework routine** that would help ensure **adequate completion of all assigned work** and improve chances of academic success. **(P,N)**

- _____ uses his/her planner **only when directed to do so** by the teacher and **usually completes homework on time**. _____ is **encouraged to** work on **organizational skills** and **utilize class time more effectively**. **(N,P)**

Negative

- _____ is encouraged **to bring** his/her organizer **daily**. **(N)**

- _____ demonstrates **effective use** of his/her organizer. **(N)**

- _____ **uses** class time and his/her organizer **effectively**. **(N)**

- _____ **must use** his/her **organizer daily** to achieve success. **(N)**

- _____ has **not used** his/her organizer **as effectively** this term. **(N)**

- School organizer **needs to be used regularly**, **neatly**, and **effectively**. **(N)**

- _____ is encouraged to **bring** his/her organizer **to class daily**. **(N)**

- _____ **must make better use** of his/her organizer **on a daily basis**. **(N)**

- _____ often **neglects to complete** and **bring** organizer **to school**. **(N)**

- _____ **has not made as effective use** of his/her organizer this term. **(N)**

- School organizer is used **consistently** and **as instructed some of the time**. **(N)**

- **Homework completion** and appropriate **use** of **organizer** remain a **concern**. **(N)**

- School organizer is **used** as instructed **only with regular teacher reminders**. **(N)**

- _____ **uses** his/her **organizer** to record important dates and information. **(N)**

- _____ **needs to ensure** that the organizer **is complete** and **kept up-to-date**. **(N)**

- **Inconsistent homework completion remains a concern** and a **hindrance** to learning. **(N)**

- _____ **is encouraged** to use his/her organizer **to help with long-term** planning. **(N)**

- _____ **is encouraged to use class time** and his/her **organizer more effectively**. **(N)**

- _____ is still **encouraged** to use his/her organizer **to record all assignment due dates**. **(N)**

- School agenda **needs to be brought to class regularly**, **independently,** and **as instructed**. (**N**)

- _____ is **encouraged to use** his/her organizer and **complete all homework** tasks **daily**. (**N**)

- **Daily use** of organizer and improved work habits **would help** _____ meet daily expectations. (**N**)

- _____ is encouraged to use his/her organizer daily **in order to complete all homework tasks**. (**N**)

- School organizer is used to record homework and other important information **with teacher's assistance**. (**N**)

- _____ is still encouraged to use his/her organizer **to record all assignment due dates** and their criteria. (**N**)

- _____ **needs to use** the school organizer **on a daily basis** to monitor the work he/she has to complete. (**N**)

- A **more effective** use of his/her organizer should help _____ keep track of assignments and due dates. (**N**)

- _____ is **encouraged** to use his/her organizer **more effectively** by (_scheduling/recording_) weekly **remedial** sessions. (**N**)

- It is recommended that _____ assume **greater responsibility** for **maintenance** and **effective use of school organizer**. (**N**)

- _____ **needs reminders to use** his/her planner and **frequent** one-to-one **assistance to complete** his/her school **work**. (**N**)

- **Taking organizer home** and **setting aside regular time for homework** and reading are routines that must be adhered to on daily basis. (**N**)

- _____ is encouraged to **incorporate remedial dates** into his/her organizer in order **to address program concerns promptly**. (**N**)

- _____ **has not made as effective use** of his/her organizer this term, and is **encouraged to make improvements** in this area. (**N**)

- _____ **must learn to use the organizer as a practical tool** that reminds him/her of homework, due dates, and other important information. (**N**)

- _____ is **encouraged to use** his/her **organizer more effectively** to ensure that **assignments** and other **activities** are **completed on time**. (**N**)

- _____ **is encouraged** to take his/her **organizer** home each day and **set aside regular time** for completion of **homework** assignments and reading. (**N**)

- _____ **must accept responsibility for recording homework** and long-term **assignments** in his/her organizer and for **completing tasks on time. (N)**

- _____ **needs to assume greater responsibility for** establishing and maintaining effective use of **organizer, study,** and **homework** completion **routines. (N)**

- _____ **must accept responsibility** for **recording homework** and **completing assigned tasks** on time, **relying less on others** to do this for him/her. (**N**)

- _____ **needs to assume greater responsibility for** establishing and maintaining **effective use of organizer, study,** and **homework completion** routines. (**N**)

- _____ is (still) **encouraged** to **record detailed** and **accurate** information in his/her organizer in order **to be reminded** of daily **academic duties** and **responsibilities. (N)**

- _____ is **encouraged to use** his/her organizer **more effectively** by (*scheduling/ booking*) weekly **remedial** sessions. They will **help** ensure **timely completion and submission of assigned work. (N)**

- It is (again) recommended that _____ assume **greater responsibility** for **maintenance and effective use of school organizer,** and **development of a consistent homework** and **study routine. (N)**

- _____ must ensure that all **homework** tasks are completed on time. It is recommended that he/she **assume greater responsibility for** maintenance and **effective use of his/her school organizer,** and development of a **consistent homework routine. (N)**

- _____ **must learn to use** the **organizer as a practical tool** that reminds him/her of **homework**, due dates, and other important information. _____ is **strongly encouraged** to establish a **daily homework** routine that ensures **completion of all assigned work. (N)**

- **Homework completion** and appropriate use of **organizer** remain a **concern.** _____ is **encouraged to take** his/her **organizer home** each day and set aside regular time for completion of **homework** assignments and **reading.** All **school equipment must be brought to class daily**, ready for use and in good working condition. (**N**)

Report Card and IEP Comments

Class Participation

General

- **Ideas** and **opinions** (thoughts, feelings, knowledge, point of view) **are communicated** with (*little/ some/ much*) **clarity** and **accuracy**. (**G**)

- _____ **communicates with** (*little/ some/ much*) **clarity** and (*little/ some/ much*) **accuracy** for a wide range of (simple) purposes. (**G**)

- When participating in class, _____ **speaks with** (*little/ some/ much*) **clarity** and is able to **communicate ideas and information** (*with much teacher help/ with some assistance and guidance/ independently/ clearly and contidently*).

Positive

- _____ **responds** to questions **effectively**. (**P**)

- **Verbal communication skills** continue to **show steady gains**. (**P**)

- _____ **demonstrates interest and enthusiasm** in the classroom. (**P**)

- _____ **establishes positive relationships** with peers and teachers. (**P**)

- _____ is **getting better at listening to opinions and ideas of others**. (**P**)

- _____ **readily** and **successfully participates in** class **oral presentations**. (**P**)

- _____ **retells** personal experiences **with passion, enthusiasm, and clarity**. (**P**)

- _____ is a (*good/ very effective*) **communicator** in oral and visual assignments. (**P**)

- _____ **listens** and **does not interrupt** the class **with off-the-topic comments**. (**P**)

- _____ continues to have a **good working relationship with other students** in the class. (**P**)

- _____ is **becoming more comfortable** with **expressing** himself/herself in front of others. (**P**)

- _____ **contributes positively to class discussions** and cooperative **group activities**. (**P**)

- _____ **participates frequently** in class discussions and **volunteers opinions freely**. (**P**)

- _____ is a **very effective communicator** when participating in oral and visual assignments. **(P)**

- _____ **often participates in class** and is **willing to answer questions** and **offer suggestions**. **(P)**

- _____ is an **enthusiastic learner** who **enjoys group activities** and **socializing** with his/her peers. **(P)**

- _____ often **contributes** to class **by offering opinions** and **volunteering answers** to questions. **(P)**

- _____ **must learn to respect opinions of others** and **take responsibility for** his/her **own actions**. **(P)**

- _____ is **encouraged to remain focused** during class and **restrict comments to lesson-related topics**. **(P)**

- _____ continues to **participate** in class activities **with enthusiasm**, **motivation**, and an ever-present **smile**. **(P)**

- _____ **participates often** and shows **ability to concentrate** by **identifying main points** and **staying on topic**. **(P)**

- _____ possesses **strong leadership potential** and is encouraged to provide leadership in a variety of groupings. **(P)**

- _____ **consistently participates** in, and **often leads discussions**, and **contributes insightful questions**, **comments**, and **ideas**. **(P)**

- _____ **demonstrates an ability to pay attention** in class, **asking** and **appropriately answering** relevant **questions**. **(P)**

- **Some progress was observed**, and _____ is **to be commended** for his/her **willingness and enthusiasm to succeed** in this area. **(P)**

- _____ **participates frequently** in discussions **by actively listening**, **asking questions, considering the ideas of others**, and **making appropriate contributions**. **(P)**

- _____ **participated actively during our repeated reading sessions,** as he/she found the selected articles interesting and amusing to read. _____ is **to be commended for** his/her **willingness to read aloud** to others in class. **(P)**

Positive/Negative

- **Participates eagerly** in discussions, **but often needs reminders to settle down** and **focus** on the relevant topic. **(P,N)**

- _____ **participates** in class **often** and **with enthusiasm,** but **requires frequent reminders to concentrate** and **stay on topic**. **(P,N)**

- _____ **is able to work cooperatively** and **independently** to achieve his/her academic goals **when fully committed** to a task. (**P,N**)

- _____ **listens to others without interrupting,** and is **encouraged to participate actively** in all **class discussions** and **group activities**. (**P,N**)

- _____ **continues to improve** in this area **but at a slower pace**. **Verbal interruptions** and **negativity** are **hindering learning** (growth). (**P,N**)

- _____ **participates eagerly** in group discussions **but has difficulty with knowing when to talk**, **when to listen,** and **how much to say**. (**P,N**)

- _____ **often contributes to class discussions with enthusiasm** by offering opinions and volunteering answers to questions; **however, ideas** and **opinions** are **communicated unclearly**. (**P,N**)

- _____ is an **enthusiastic learner** who **enjoys group activities** and **socializing** with peers. He/she is **encouraged to work on reviewing concepts** in subject areas which may be a challenge to him/her. (**P,N**)

- _____ has **enjoyed presenting in front of the class** and (*always/ usually*) **volunteers** to be the first. **Forming long sentences** and **presenting ideas in logical order** are **still** areas where there is **room for further growth** and **improvement**. (**P,N**)

- _____ participated in several **presentations** to the class. He/she is **encouraged to participate more** by **asking and answering questions** to obtain and clarify information, and **express** and **respond** to a range of ideas and opinions. (**P,N**)

- _____ often **volunteers to answer questions** during class discussions; however, **frequent distractibility is at times a hindrance** to successful and appropriate communication with teachers and peers. **Ideas and opinions** are **communicated with some clarity** and some precision. (**P,N**)

- _____ is **becoming more comfortable** with **expressing** himself/herself in front of others. **Learning strategies** such as, **drama, echo speaking, retelling of information** in own words, **giving "waiting time,"** and **supporting classroom environment are helping** _____ make some progress in this area. (**P,N**)

- _____ **often participates in class** and is **willing to answer questions** and **offer suggestions;** however, **limited ability to concentrate and stay on topic make clear communication difficult**. _____ is **encouraged to make a conscious effort to speak at a slower** pace, focusing on **clear and accurate enunciation** of words. (**P,N**)

- _____ is **getting better at listening to opinions and ideas of others**. In order to avoid unnecessary **arguments** with classmates, it is **important** for _____ to learn **when it is appropriate to interrupt and for how long to speak. Keeping conversations light** and **positive** would help encourage and promote constructive and healthy relationships with peers. (**P,N**)

- Although _____ still **needs to learn to project** his/her **voice** when speaking, he/she has **clearly improved in this area**. **(N,P)**

Negative

- **Frequent distractibility** and lack of focus are a serious concern. **(N)**

- **Speech** continues to be presented **in short phrases** or **single words**. **(N)**

- _____ is **encouraged** to participate more in **class discussions**. **(N)**

- _____ **contributes** information and **ideas** to the class and group. **(N)**

- _____ is **encouraged** to take a more **active role** in class sessions. **(N)**

- _____ is **encouraged** to **contribute** more in **large group** sessions. **(N)**

- _____ has **difficulty expressing ideas in a clear** and **concise manner**. **(N)**

- **Ideas and opinions** are **communicated with some clarity** and some precision. **(N)**

- _____ **maintains** a **very good working relationship** with other students. **(N)**

- _____ **speaks rarely** and when he/she does, it is **often done out of impulse**. **(N)**

- **Better concentration** in class **would improve achievement** in this and other areas. **(N)**

- _____ is **often unwilling to bend** and **compromise during group activities**. **(N)**

- _____ is **encouraged to volunteer and express** his/her **opinion** in class **more often**. **(N)**

- _____ is **encouraged to volunteer answers** and **participate orally more often** in class. **(N)**

- _____ is **continuing to work on developing socially acceptable interaction** with others. **(N)**

- _____ continues to **enunciate words quickly**, and is often **difficult to understand**. **(N)**

- _____ **still speaks out of impulse**, with **limited sense of when to speak** and **for how long**. **(N)**

- **Forming sentences** and **presenting ideas in a logical order** are **still** areas with **room for improvement**. **(N)**

- _____ is **encouraged to contribute more information** and **ideas** to class and group discussions. **(N)**

- Cooperative **group lessons are very difficult to conduct** when _____ is **not focused** on the activity. (**N**)

- **Keeping conversations light** and **positive** would help encourage and promote constructive and healthy **relationships** with **peers**. (**N**)

- _____ **engaged** this term **in fewer oral discussions** and was **noticeably less willing** to express **ideas** and **opinions**. (**N**)

- _____ is **reminded** that he/she **must concentrate on** his/her **own work** and progress, and **not on others around** him/her. (**N**)

- **Regular reading**, **writing,** and **increased knowledge of the English language are essential** for improving **communication skills**. (**N**)

- **When** things **don't turn out as expected,** _____ is encouraged to **resist the temptation to vocalize displeasure** to the entire class. (**N**)

- _____ **is encouraged to participate more frequently** in class discussions and continue to ask questions in order to clarify his/her thinking. (**N**)

- _____ **continues to struggle with appropriate social** skills in class. He/she is **eager to interact** with other students, **but often does it in a negative manner**. (**N**)

- _____'s **participation in discussions** by actively listening, asking questions, considering the ideas of others, and making appropriate contributions **is inconsistent**. (**N**)

- In order to avoid unnecessary arguments with classmates, **it is important** for _____ to learn **when it is appropriate to interrupt and for how long to speak**. (**N**)

- _____ is **encouraged to participate more** by **asking and answering questions** to obtain and clarify information and **express** and **respond** to a range of ideas and opinions. (**N**)

- _____ **sometimes gets involved in class discussions** and **shares** his/her **opinions, knowledge,** and **views**. He/she is **encouraged to volunteer answers** and **participate orally more often**. (**N**)

- _____ **communicates with some clarity,** for a variety of simple purposes. _____ **engaged** this term **in fewer oral discussions** and was **noticeably less willing** to express **ideas** and **opinions**. (**N**)

- _____ **needs to listen to others** and **work more cooperatively in a group**. It is important to **stick to the task at hand, adhering to time lines**. During the **Literature Circle** discussions, _____ would participate initially and then **need encouragement to remain involved**. He/she was **often inflexible and uncompromising during group activities**. (**N**)

- _____ **must make more effective use of class time** and **avoid distractions**. (**N,N**)

Report Card and IEP Comments

- **Interrupting the lesson** or other presenters **takes away from the flow** of classroom activities. (**N,N**)

- _____ is **often speaking out of turn**, **without regard for the needs of others** in the class. (**N,N**)

- _____ is **encouraged to stay focused** during class time, and **not become distracted**. (**N,N**)

- **Nonstop distractibility often** (seriously/ greatly) **hinders communication** with teacher and others. (**N,N**)

- _____ **has a limited sense of when to end verbal communication** with his/her teachers and peers. (**N,N**)

- _____ is **encouraged to seek positive relationships** and to **interact in an appropriate fashion**. (**N,N**)

- **Demonstrating a sense of when to speak**, **when to listen**, and **how much to say remains a challenge**. (**N,N**)

- **Frequent distractibility** and **lack of focus** are having a very negative impact on academic achievement. (**N,N**)

- **Distractibility** often (frequently) **prevents successful** and **appropriate communication** with teachers and peers. (**N,N**)

- _____ often appears to **speak out of impulse**, with a **limited sense of when to speak** and **for how long**. (**N,N**)

- _____ **needs regular reminders regarding socially appropriate interaction** and **courtesy toward others**. (**N,N**)

- _____ **needs to assume greater responsibility for focusing** and **attention** during class instructional periods. (**N,N**)

- **Inability to remain focused and follow instructions has had an impact on** _____'s **academic progress**. (**N,N**)

- **When things don't turn out as expected**, _____ **is encouraged to resist the temptation to vocalize displeasure** to the entire class. (**N,N**)

- **Before interrupting**, _____ is **encouraged to become a more focused listener**, giving others a chance to fully express their opinion. (**N,N**)

- Despite enthusiastic participation in class, _____ **often speaks out of impulse, with a limited sense of when to speak and for how long**. (**N,N**)

- **Frequent distractibility** and **lack of focus** often prevent (hinder/ inhibit) successful communication (interaction) with teachers and peers. (**N,N**)

- _____ **needs to show more regard for the rights and needs of others**, by respecting their personal space and by listening, participating, and taking turns. **(N,N)**

- _____ often **speaks out of impulse, with a limited sense of when to speak, and for how long. Frequent distractibility** and **lack of focus** are a **serious concern. (N,N)**

- _____ is easily **distracted**. He/she **needs** constant **encouragement** to **stay focused** on the task at hand. _____ is reminded that he/she **must concentrate on** his/her **own work** and progress, and **not on others around** him/her. **(N,N)**

- _____ often **speaks out of impulse, with a limited sense of when to speak, and for how long. Frequent distractibility** and lack of focus (is a **major concern/ have often hindered** successful communication with teachers and peers). **(N,N)**

- _____ **continues to work** on **developing socially acceptable interaction** with others. **Negative comments** are **occasionally directed toward peers.**_____ is **encouraged to seek positive relationships** and **interact appropriately. (N,N)**

- _____ **needs regular reminders regarding socially appropriate interaction** and **courtesy** toward others. He/she **often speak out of turn, without regard for the needs of others** in the class. He/she **needs to show more regard for the rights and needs of others** by **respecting their personal space** and listening to what others have to say as well. **(N,N)**

Report Card and IEP Comments

Group Work

General

- _____ shows (*little/ some/ good/ excellent*) **ability** to **work independently in groups**. **(G)**

Positive

- _____ **shows interest** and **enthusiasm** in the classroom. **(P)**

- _____ **forms positive relationships** with classroom peers and teachers. **(P)**

- _____ **listens** and **does not interrupt** the class **with off-the-topic comments**. **(P)**

- _____ **contributes positively to class discussions** and **cooperative group activities**. **(P)**

- _____ is an **enthusiastic learner** who **enjoys group activities** and **socializing** with his/her peers. **(P)**

- _____ **participates in group discussion**, **using appropriate language** and **complete sentences**. **(P)**

- **Some progress was observed**, and _____ is to be commended for his/her **willingness and enthusiasm to succeed**. **(P)**

- _____ **interacts with** his/her **peers** during unstructured learning times **with more confidence**, and **without encouragement**. He/she **contributes ideas in a small class setting when** he/she feels that his/her opinion **needs to be heard**. **(P)**

Positive/Negative

- _____ is often **observed leading group activities**, but at times **needs reminders to focus** on the assigned goal and **give others a chance to speak**. **(P,N)**

- _____ **continues to improve** in this area **but at a slower pace. Verbal interruptions** and **negativity** are **hindering learning**. **(P,N)**

- _____ **continues to struggle with appropriate social skills** in class. He/she is **eager to interact with other students**, but it is **often done in a negative manner**. **(P,N)**

- _____ **sometimes gets involved** in **group work** and **shares** his/her **opinions, knowledge**, and **views**. He/she is encouraged to volunteer answers and participate orally more often. **(P,N)**

- _____ **sometimes gets involved** in **group work** and **shares** his/her **opinions, knowledge, views**, and **feelings**. **(N,P)**

Negative

- **Negative comments** are **occasionally (**often/ always**) directed toward peers**. **(N)**

- **Better concentration** in class **would improve achievement** in this and other areas. **(N)**

- _____ **finds it difficult to listen** during instructional time and group discussions. **(N)**

- _____ **continues to work** on **developing socially acceptable interaction** with others. **(N)**

- _____ is **encouraged to listen** patiently to **opinions** of others and wait for his/her turn to speak. **(N)**

- _____ is **encouraged to contribute more information** and **ideas** to class and group discussions. **(N)**

- _____ is **encouraged to seek positive relationships** with others, and **interact in an appropriate fashion**. **(N)**

- _____ is **encouraged to resist the temptation to vocalize displeasure to the entire class** when things don't turn out as expected. **(N)**

- _____ is **encouraged to participate in class and group activities**, and **ask questions to clarify meaning** and **ensure understanding**. **(N)**

- _____ **will interact** and contribute **in small groups with others who initiate contact** with him/her. However, he/she is **quite reluctant to initiate contact** on his/her own **when group work is assigned**. **(N)**

- _____ **continues to experience difficulty with appropriate social interaction and conduct** with students in our class. He/she is encouraged to continue working on developing a greater understanding toward the needs of his/her peers. **(N)**

- _____ **continues to work** on **developing socially acceptable interaction** with others. **Negative comments** are **occasionally directed toward peers**. _____ is **encouraged to seek positive relationships** with others, and **interact in an appropriate fashion**. **(N)**

- **Frequent distractibility** and **lack of focus** are a **(major/serious) concern**. **(N,N)**

- _____ **continues to struggle with appropriate social skills** in class. **(N,N)**

Report Card and IEP Comments

- **Frequent distractibility** and **lack of focus** are affecting academic achievement. (**N,N**)

- **Interruptions of lessons and answers of classmates** take away from the flow of classroom activities. (**N,N**)

- **Distractibility** often **prevents successful** and **appropriate communication** with teacher and peers. (**N,N**)

- Cooperative **group lessons** are **very difficult to conduct** when _____ is **not focused** on the activity. (**N,N**)

- **Inability to remain focused** and **follow instructions has had an impact on** _____'s **academic progress**. (**N,N**)

- **Frequent distractibility** and **lack of focus** often prevent (hinder/inhibit) successful communication with teachers and peers. (**N,N**)

- _____ **requires frequent reminders to conduct** himself/herself **appropriately** when interacting with others in a small group setting. (**N,N**)

- _____ **is encouraged to resist the temptation to vocalize displeasure** at the entire class **when things don't turn out as expected**. (**N,N**)

- _____ often **speaks out of impulse, with a limited sense of when to speak and for how long. Frequent distractibility** and lack of focus (is a **major concern/ have often hindered** successful participation in groups). (**N,N**)

Independent Work

General

- _____ (*rarely/ sometimes/ usually/ always*) **solves problems** without teacher assistance. (**G**)

- _____ (*rarely/ sometimes/ usually/ always*) **follows classroom (school) routines** and **instructions independently**. (**G**)

- _____ **shows** (*little/ some/ good/ excellent*) **ability** to **work** independently **in groups**. (**G**)

- _____ follows **classroom (school) routines** and **instructions** (*with teacher assistance/ with some assistance/ independently*). (**G**)

Positive

- _____ is a **focused** and **self-motivated** student. (**P,P**)

- _____ consistently **uses** his/her **time effectively** and **remains on task**. (**P,P**)

- _____ shows **effective time management** and **organizational skills**. (**P,P**)

- _____ **approaches new challenges** and **tasks with motivation**, **eagerness**, and **confidence**. (**P,P**)

- _____ **works** well **independently** and is **consistently on task**. He/she demonstrates **self-direction** in learning. (**P,P**)

- _____ shows **motivation** and **self-confidence**. He/she **consistently uses** his/her **time effectively** and **remains on task**. (**P,P**)

- _____ shows **self-direction** in learning. (**P**)

- _____ shows **motivation** and **self-confidence**. (**P**)

- _____ **works** well **independently** and is **on task consistently**. (**P**)

- _____ **works well independently** and **shows self-motivation**. (**P**)

- _____ (usually) obtains and investigates **information** independently. (**P**)

- _____ **consistently seeks work** and **new opportunities for learning**. (**P**)

- _____ shows **self-direction** in learning and (usually/ always) completes **homework on time** and with care. (**P**)

Report Card and IEP Comments

- _____ possesses **strong leadership potential** and is encouraged to provide leadership in a variety of groupings. (**P**)

- _____ **works well independently** and is **beginning to feel more comfortable when** working **in unfamiliar group settings**. (**P**)

- **Some progress was observed**, and _____ is to be commended for his/her **willingness and enthusiasm to succeed**. (**P**)

- _____ **works well independently**, shows **good motivation,** and is a **risk taker**, especially when working on tasks that require **problem solving** and **creativity**. (**P**)

- _____ shows **self-direction** in learning, and usually completes **homework on time** and with care. He/she **usually investigates** and obtains **information** independently. (**P**)

Positive/Negative

- _____ continues to **work well independently**, but **has had some difficulty working in groups**. (**P,N**)

- _____ follows **routines** and **instructions independently**. _____ sometimes **solves problems** without assistance. (**P,N**)

- _____ **continues to improve** in this area **but at a slower pace**. Verbal interruptions and negativity are hindering learning. (**P,N**)

- _____ is **able** to work **cooperatively** and **independently** to achieve his/her academic goals **when fully committed to a task**. (**N,P**)

- _____ approaches new challenges and tasks with **motivation**, eagerness, and **confidence**. _____ is able to use **information** and **technology** systems **effectively** and has, consequently, **experienced a good deal of success** this term. He/she **willingly accepts various roles** within the class **and group situations**, including the role of a **leader**. (**N,P**)

Negative

- **Better concentration** in class **would improve achievement** in this and other areas. (**N**)

- _____ shows **effective time management** and **organizational skills.** (**N**)

- **Interrupting the lesson**, or **other speakers**, takes away from the flow of classroom activities. (**N**)

- **Distractibility** often (frequently/ usually/ always) prevents successful and appropriate communication with teachers and peers. (**N**)

- _____ is **encouraged to resist the temptation to vocalize displeasure to the entire class** when things don't turn out as expected. (**N**)

Initiative

Positive

- _____ is a **highly motivated** student who **participates** in class activities **with creativity** and **great deal of enthusiasm**. (P, P)

- _____ is a **highly motivated** student who **participates** in class activities **with creativity** and **great deal of enthusiasm**. His/her willingness to **lead, organize,** and **inspire** others is **well noted**. (P, P)

- _____'s willingness to **lead, organize,** and **inspire** others is **well noted**. (P)

- _____ **consistently seeks work** and **new opportunities** for **learning**. (P)

- _____ **participates well** in class and **begins tasks** of his/her **own initiative**. (P)

- _____ shows **effective time management** and **organizational skills**. (P)

- _____ possesses **strong leadership potential** and is encouraged to provide leadership in a variety of groupings. (P)

- _____ **works** well **independently** and is **consistently on task**. He/she shows **self-direction** in learning. (P)

- **Some progress was observed**, and _____ is **to be commended** for his/her **willingness and enthusiasm to succeed**. (P)

- _____ **shows motivation** and **self-confidence**. He/she **puts forth a consistent effort** and **seeks positive solutions to conflict**. (P)

- _____ is a **motivated, happy** learner who **enjoys being with** his/her **peers** and working on group projects. _____ **participates well** in class. (P)

- _____ **works well independently, shows good motivation** and is a **risk taker**, especially when working on tasks that require **problem solving** and **creativity**. (P)

- _____ is a **considerate** and **energetic** student who has **adjusted** (fairly) **well** to the **routines** and **expectations** of our classroom. His/her **willingness to lead and organize** class **activities** is **noted** and **appreciated**. (P)

Positive/Negative

- _____ **shows motivation, initiative,** and **self-direction**. He/she is **encouraged to accurately analyze** and **assess** the **value of information**. (P,N)

- _____ has **expressed an eagerness to do better** in the area of **academics** this term; however, **difficulty in reaching some of his/her goals was experienced** throughout the term. **(P,N)**

Negative

- _____ is **encouraged to show motivation** and **initiative,** and **contribute to cooperative problem solving**. **(N)**

- _____ is **reminded to put forth initiative toward** all **written work** in order to experience further success. **(N)**

- _____ **needs to improve** his/her **level of commitment** and **concentration** on **daily tasks** and on **long-term assignments**. **(N)**

- _____ **needs to assume greater responsibility for being prepared for class,** with notes and **materials** readily available to commence work. **(N)**

- _____ demonstrates lack of **self-direction** in learning and **rarely completes homework on time** and **with care**. He/she rarely **investigates** and **obtains information independently**. **(N)**

Problem Solving

General

- _____ (*rarely/ sometimes/ usually/ always*) **solves problems** independently. (**G**)

- _____ (*with teacher assistance/ with some assistance/ independently*) **modifies** or **invents** (thinks of) **strategies** for problem solving. (**G**)

Positive

- _____ **often interprets** and **understands problems**. (**P**)

- **Some progress was observed**, and _____ is **to be commended** for his/her **willingness and enthusiasm to succeed**. (**P**)

- _____ **shows motivation** and **self-confidence**. He/she **puts forth** a **consistent effort** and **seeks positive solutions to conflict**. (**P**)

- _____ **seeks** (concrete/ positive/ workable/ possible) **solutions to problems** and often **solves problems without teacher assistance**. (**P**)

- _____ **perseveres through challenging tasks** and (usually/always) **tries** hard to follow through with the recommended **problem-solving process**. (**P**)

- _____ **works well independently**, shows **good motivation,** and is a **risk taker**, especially when working on tasks that require creative **problem solving**. (**P**)

- _____ **makes a good effort** on problem-solving assignments. He/she is **encouraged to persevere** and **discuss** his/her **reasoning** with peers or adults. (**P**)

Positive/Negative

- _____ **follows routines** and **instructions independently**. He/she **sometimes solves problems independently**. (**P,N**)

- _____ **continues to improve** in this area, **but at a slower pace. Verbal interruptions** and **negativity** by _____ **are hindering learning**. (**P,N**)

Negative

- _____ is encouraged to show **motivation** and contribute **to cooperative problem solving** in class. (**N**)

Report Card and IEP Comments

Goal Setting to Improve Work

Positive

- **A positive change** in **attitude** and a **desire to set goals** and **improve** are **evident**. (**P**)

- _____ **has set goals** for his/her own achievement and is **working responsibly to attain them**. (**P**)

- **Some progress was observed**, and _____ is **to be commended** for his/her **willingness and enthusiasm to do well**. (**P**)

- _____ **has set some personal goals for** his/her **programs**, especially in the area of **reading expectations**. A more conscientious individual, _____ **has set goals** for his/her own achievement and is **working diligently to attain them**. (**P**)

Positive/Negative

- _____ has expressed an **eagerness to do better** in his/her academics, **yet** he/she **has had some difficulty reaching** some of his/her **goals**. (**P,N**)

- _____ is **developing greater self-control** in all work situations, and has **established realistic goals** for himself/herself for the next term. (**P,N**)

- _____ **continues to improve** in this area **but at a slower pace**. Verbal interruptions and negativity by _____ are hindering learning in class. (**P,N**)

- _____ **has made a number of positive gains in many areas of learning skills** this term. He/she **is learning to work independently**, without interrupting his/her peers, and **more homework** assignments **have been completed** than in the past. **Remaining on task** for extended periods of time **is difficult** for _____; **however**, a **positive change** in **attitude** and a **desire to improve** are **evident**. (**P,N**)

Negative

- _____ is **encouraged to assess** his/her **own work and identify goals** toward which to strive. (**N**)

- _____ is **encouraged to put forth greater effort** in order **to accomplish goals** for himself/herself. (**N**)

- _____ is **reminded to work toward** his/her **personal best** and **refrain from socializing**, when being on task is expected. (**N**)

- _____ **needs to improve** his/her **level of commitment** and **concentration** on **daily tasks** and **long-term assignments**. (**N**)

- _____ **needs to assume greater responsibility for being prepared** for class with notes and **materials** readily available to commence work. **(N)**

- Lack of **motivation**, frequent **verbal interruptions,** and **inability to work quietly** in class are **preventing** _____ from **reaching** his/her full **academic potential. (N)**

- _____ is **encouraged to concentrate on achieving** his/her **personal goals** for the final **term, including a more risk-taking approach** to new and challenging learning situations. **(N)**

- _____ was not able to demonstrate an understanding of the materials covered in class as he/she **did not begin** or **complete any** (most) **class assignments. (N)**

- _____ **did not seek additional assistance although this option was offered** to him/her on a daily basis (throughout the term). **(N)**

Attending and Concentrating

General/Negative

- _____ (*rarely/ sometimes/ often/ usually/ always*) **follows oral instructions** (*but/ and*) continues to have **difficulty maintaining concentration** and **focus, especially if other distractions are present** in the room. (**G,N**)

- _____ (*usually/ often*) **follows oral instructions but continues to have** (some) **difficulty maintaining concentration**, especially **when other distractions are present** in the room. Making a conscious effort to ignore such distractions would help. (**G,N**)

General/Negative/Positive

- _____ (*rarely/ sometimes/ often/ usually/ always*) **follows oral instructions** (*but/ and*) **continues to have difficulty maintaining concentration** and **focus**, especially if other distractions are present in the room. He/she is **encouraged to make a conscious effort to ignore** such **distractions. When working in a small** cooperative **group setting** _____ **often assists others who need help and** assumes the role of a leader. (**G,N,P**)

Positive

- This **no longer seems to be an area of need** for _____. _____ **focuses well** in class and **always follows oral** (teacher) **instructions.** _____ has become much **better at making and maintaining eye contact.** (**P,P**)

- _____ **shows** (an) **ability to pay attention** in class. (**P**)

- _____ **is to be congratulated** for **improving** his/her **ability to attend** and **concentrate** in class. _____ **worked quietly** and **diligently** most of the time this term, which contributed to his/her (consistent and) **improved academic achievement.** (**P**)

- **Change in seating plan** has helped _____ **concentrate** more effectively on given tasks. (**P**)

- _____ is **showing increased willingness to focus** and **complete assigned work** in class. (**P**)

- With a **change in seating** arrangements, _____ **has been able to get more** of his/ her **work done.** (**P**)

- _____ is **to be congratulated** for **improving** his/her **ability to attend** and **concentrate** in class. (**P**)

- _____ **demonstrates an ability to pay attention** in class, **asking** and **appropriately answering** relevant **questions**. (**P**)

- He/she **is learning to use** his/her **time effectively** and **prioritize** his/her **tasks to ensure that learning assignments** are **completed**. (**P**)

- **Some progress was observed**, and _____ is **to be commended** for his/her **willingness** and **enthusiasm to succeed** (do well). (**P**)

- _____ is to be **congratulated** for **improving** his/her **ability to attend** and **concentrate** in class. _____ **worked quietly** and **diligently** most of the time this term, which contributed to a **fruitful learning environment**. (**P**)

Positive/Negative

- _____ **often participates in class** and is **willing to answer questions** and **offer suggestions**; however, **limited ability to concentrate** and **stay on topic** make clear **communication difficult**. _____ is **encouraged** to **make a conscious effort** to **speak at a slower** pace, focusing on **clear and accurate enunciation** of words. (**P,N**)

- _____ **continues to improve** in this area **but at a slower pace. Verbal interruptions** and **negativity** by _____ are **hindering learning**. (**P,N**)

- **With reminders to stay focused** and a **change in seating arrangements**, _____ is **beginning to respond** by being more **attentive** in class. (**N,P**)

- _____ **has tried** this term **to be an active participant** during instructional periods. **However,** he/she **often requires reminders to position** himself/herself in a way that is conducive to a better **learning environment**. (**P,N**)

- _____ is **making an effort to exercise self-control** in class. **When frustrated,** or **overly excited, this becomes** a **very difficult task.** It usually **takes a long time** to **get settled** and **participate constructively** in class. (**P,N**)

- **Being seated at the front** of the class **assists** _____ **with attention and concentration.** He/she **usually follows instructions, but requires extra time to respond.** _____ **benefits from having a written copy** of what is being read. (**P,N**)

- _____ **continues to make some progress** by not allowing comments by others to interfere with his/her **focus, work,** and **concentration** in class. _____ is **encouraged to look for the positive sides of classmates**, and not point out and **dwell on the negative.** (**P,N**)

- _____ is **becoming more aware** of the fact that **raising** his/her **hand is a polite and orderly way of signaling that** he/she **has a question to ask** or an **opinion to express.** _____ is **making an observable, conscious effort to ignore distractions** around him/her. (**P,N**)

- _____ works best when seated in a place with **minimal distractions**. When working in a **group setting**, _____ **often assists others who need help**. **Giving** _____ **a chance to answer questions** and **show examples on the blackboard** has **increased** his/her motivation to concentrate and learn. (**P,N**)

- _____ is **able to work and focus well in a small group** or one-to-one situation. He/she is, **however**, **experiencing difficulty behaving** in an appropriate manner **during regular class**. He/she **often interrupts lessons without regard for others**. **Habitual** (persistent/ frequent/ recurring/ periodic) **distractibility** and **lack of focus** are a **concern**. (**P,N**)

- _____ is an extremely **enthusiastic** and **active participant** in all of our class activities. _____ **at times needs reminders to** go back to his/her desk and **reduce the amount of socializing** during class. **Increased concentration** on school work and **more consistent performance in class** would help improve achievement in many areas of the curriculum. (**P,N**)

- During class **discussions** _____ **frequently engages** and is an **active, contributing member. When working individually** or **in a small group, however,** he/she **requires** gentle **verbal cues** and **reminders to continue working. When** he/she is **working on an assignment of interest,** and **in a positive frame of mind,** he/she **is able to complete assignments well.** _____ **needs to recognize when** he/she is **off task** and begin to pull himself/herself back to constructive participation and learning. (**P,N**)

- _____ **partakes actively** and **enthusiastically in many** of our **class activities.** He/she **has been a positive influence** on the **study habits of other classmates** as he/she **enjoys teaming up with** his/her **peers** and **rehearsing for tests. At times** _____ **gets overly excited** and **needs to be reminded to quietly focus** on a given task. (**P,N**)

- **Remaining on task for extended periods of time is difficult** for _____; however, a **positive change in attitude** and a **desire to improve** are **evident.** (**N,P**)

- **Some improvement in completing tasks was observed**; however, **distractibility** and **frequent verbal** lesson **interruptions remain a serious concern.** (**N,P**)

- _____ **requires teacher prompts to initiate tasks.** He/she **is learning to use** his/her **time effectively** and **prioritize** his/her **tasks to ensure that learning assignments are completed.** (**N,P**)

- _____ **allows small distractions** and **comments by others to interfere with focus and concentration** in class. **With** teacher **assistance** and regular reminders, **progress continues to be made** in this area. (**N,P**)

- _____ is **making an effort not to allow small distractions and comments** by others **to interfere with focus and concentration** in class. **With** teacher **assistance,** and regular reminders, **progress continues to be made** in this area. (**N,P**)

- _____ **demonstrates an eagerness to do well,** yet **does not always follow through with commitment.** _____ **has a tendency to distract** himself/herself and others, and is **experiencing difficulty using class time wisely.** It is recommended that

_____ **focus on own efforts, rather than those of others** in order to experience greater success. **(N,P)**

Negative

- _____ **requires teacher prompts to initiate tasks**. **(N)**

- **Greater degree of self-control** during lessons **must be exercised**. **(N)**

- **Frequent distractibility** and **lack of focus continue to be a concern**. **(N)**

- _____ is **experiencing difficulty behaving** appropriately during class. **(N)**

- **Better concentration** in class **would improve achievement** in this and other areas. **(N)**

- _____ **finds it difficult to listen** during instructional time and group discussions. **(N)**

- _____ **needs frequent reminders not to interrupt** and to **remain focused** and on task. **(N)**

- **Interrupting the lesson** or other speakers **takes away from the flow** of classroom activities. **(N)**

- **Less socializing** and **greater concentration would produce** even **greater results** in this course. **(N)**

- _____ **needs** frequent **reminders to stay focused** and **refrain from interrupting**. **(N)**

- _____ is **encouraged to listen** patiently to **opinions** of others and wait for his/her turn to speak. **(N)**

- _____ often **interrupts lessons without regard for others** or for the **consequences**. **(N)**

- _____ is **encouraged to focus** on tasks and **make an effort to complete** all **work** as instructed. **(N)**

- When working in **small groups**, _____ **requires much assistance** with **remaining on task**. **(N)**

- _____ **needs frequent reminders to begin** his/her work, **focus** on a given activity, and **remain on task**. **(N)**

- **Habitual** (persistent/ frequent/ recurring/ periodic) **distractibility** and **lack of focus** are affecting academic achievement. **(N)**

- _____ **works best on a one-to-one basis**. He/she is able to concentrate and experience success at these times. **(N)**

- **Inability to remain focused and follow instructions has had an impact on** _____'s **academic progress**. (**N**)

- **Distractibility** often (frequently/ usually) **prevents** _____'s **successful** and **appropriate communication** with teachers and peers. (**N**)

- _____ is **encouraged to resist the temptation to vocalize displeasure to the entire class** when things don't turn out as expected. (**N**)

- **Focusing on work** and **given tasks, while ignoring other distractions, will help** _____ improve his/her quality of work and academic achievement. (**N**)

- **Habitual** (persistent/ frequent/ recurring/ periodic) **distractibility** and **lack of focus** often **prevent** (hinder/ inhibit) **successful communication** with teachers and peers. (**N**)

- _____ is **often observed wandering around** (roaming/ roving about) **the classroom, starting conversations** that **distract** from doing the required work. (**N**)

- _____ is **encouraged to spend more time being focused** and **attentive** during instructional periods in order to fully grasp important details and information. (**N**)

- _____ is **experiencing some difficulty behaving** appropriately during class, and **often has difficulty controlling** his/her **emotional outbursts**. (**N**)

- When confronted with **frustrating situations,** _____ is **encouraged to deal with them by using the practical problem-solving strategies** and the **stop, think method**. (**N**)

- **Inconsistent performance, effort,** and **focus upon learning are hindering academic growth.** _____ **needs to follow the teacher's instructions** and improve classroom **work habits**. (**N**)

- _____ **needs reminders to begin tasks and attend** to assigned activities. He/she is **often observed wandering around the classroom,** starting conversations that distract from doing the required work. (**N**)

- _____ **continues to require much assistance with remaining on task. Distractibility in the form of wandering** (roaming/ roving about) and **speaking to others** during lessons **is hindering learning**. (**N**)

- _____ **has difficulty adjusting to the routines and expectations** of the classroom. He/she **has difficulty cooperating in small groups** and **requires much assistance** during **independent work time**. (**N**)

- _____ **can follow oral instructions** but at times **has difficulty maintaining concentration,** especially if other **distractions** are present in the room. **Making a conscious effort to ignore** these distractions **would help**. (**N**)

- _____ is **encouraged to listen** and **consider ideas** of others without **interrupting** and **being negative. Frequent vocal complaints** and **negative comments** continue to **undermine** the classroom learning environment. (**N**)

- _____ is **encouraged to listen** patiently to **opinions** of others and **wait for** his/her **turn to speak. Interrupting** lessons **by regularly getting out of** his/her **seat** and **speaking out of turn** continue to be a **serious hindrance** to learning for _____. (**N**)

- _____ is **often in haste to complete work** and consequently **makes careless errors** in assigned tasks. **By listening**, and **starting** only **when instructed** to do so, task completion will have a greater chance of being done accurately. (**N**)

- _____ **sometimes follows oral instructions** but continues **to have difficulty maintaining concentration and focus**, especially **if other distractions are present** in the room. He/she is encouraged to make a conscious effort to **ignore** such **distractions**. (**N**)

- _____ **works best** in a **setting with minimal distractions. When** _____ is **interested** in the topic at hand, he/she **can be focused** for **short periods** of time. He/she **requires support during large group discussions**. (**N**)

- _____ **still needs reminders to remain focused** and **on task**. He/she **allows small distractions** and **comments** by others **to interfere with focus and concentration. With** teacher **assistance** and regular reminders, progress **can be made** in this area. (**N**)

- _____ 's **attention span is frequently sporadic**, and he/she is **often preoccupied with material unrelated to the lesson** at hand. He/she is encouraged to continue working on development of **skills** and **habits** that lead to greater degree of **concentration** during instructional periods. (**N**)

- **Greater degree of self-control** during lessons **must be exercised**. When confronted with **frustrating situations**, _____ is encouraged to deal with them by using the **practical problem-solving strategies** and the **stop**, **think method**. _____ **will** continue to receive assistance in this area. (**N**)

- _____ **continues to have difficulty following teacher instructions** and (very) **often needs reminders to begin tasks** and see them to completion. _____ is **generally observed wandering** (roaming/ roving about) **around the classroom, starting conversations** during lessons and **interrupting the learning of others**. (**N**)

- _____ **does not always follow teacher instructions** and at times **needs encouragement to begin tasks** and **see them to completion. Lack of motivation** is getting in the way of his/her learning. _____ is **encouraged to make a greater effort to focus in class**, as this usually translates into tangible academic achievement. (**N**)

- This term, _____ **continued to experience difficulty focusing** on the task at hand. He/she **finds it difficult to listen** during instructional time and group discussions. He/she **prefers to chat** with whoever is sitting beside him/her at the time. _____ **needs to** continue to **work on paying attention** to the appropriate auditory stimuli in the classroom. (**N**)

- _____ is **experiencing some difficulty behaving** in an appropriate manner during class, and **often has difficulty controlling** his/her **emotional outbursts**. _____ **needs frequent reminders not to interrupt** and to remain focused and on task. **With** teacher

Report Card and IEP Comments

support and **guidance**, as well as a **social skills program**, it is hoped that _____ will soon experience improvement in this area. (**N**)

- _____ is **encouraged to listen** patiently to **opinions** of others and **wait for** his/her **turn to speak. Interrupting lessons** or **other speakers by making comments, getting out of seat**, and **speaking out of turn** takes away from the flow of classroom activities. _____ **continues to wander around the class** a great deal, **visiting** others and **striking up conversations**, during lessons. While **socializing** with classmates is a good thing, it is important that _____ make a greater commitment to **staying on task** and **focusing** on learning activities. (**N**)

- _____ **still needs reminders to remain focused** and **on task. Following** classroom **routines, complaining less**, and **meeting the behavioral expectations would help** _____ attend to task at hand and meet the academic challenges of our program with more success. _____ **allows small distractions** and **comments by others to interfere with focus and concentration** in class. **With** teacher **assistance** and regular reminders, **progress is being made** in this area. (**N**)

- **Demonstrating a sense of when to speak, when to listen**, and **how much to say remains a challenge**. (**N,N**)

- **Inconsistency in attitude** and classroom **behavior** necessary for further growth **continue to hinder progress**. (**N,N**)

- **Restlessness, complaining**, and frequent/spontaneous **verbal interruptions continue to interfere with daily learning**. (**N,N**)

- **Not** (*attending/paying attention*) **and concentrating** in class, **distracting others**, and **interrupting continually** are **serious concerns**. (**N,N**)

- _____ **often interrupts** lessons **without regard for others. Frequent distractibility** and **lack of focus are a serious concern**s. (**N,N**)

- **Lack of motivation**, frequent **verbal interruptions**, and **inability to work quietly** in class **are preventing** _____ **from reaching** his/her **full academic potential**. (**N,N**)

- **Habitual** (persistent/ frequent/ recurring/ periodic) **distractibility and lack of focus are a concern**. Cooperative **group lessons** are very **difficult to conduct** when _____ is not focused on the activity. (**N,N**)

- _____ **experiences a lot of** (much) **difficulty maintaining attention** during instructional periods. He/she needs to be **attentive to teacher visual** and **verbal cues** when his/her attention begins to drift. (**N,N**)

- _____ is **experiencing difficulty behaving** in an appropriate manner during class. _____ **often interrupts** lessons **without regard for others. Habitual** (persistent/ frequent/ recurring/ periodic) **distractibility** and **lack of focus are a concern**. (**N,N**)

- _____ is **(often) easily distracted** by others around him/her **despite verbal cues** by the teacher **and reminders** to stay focused. **Tasks** are more likely to be completed on time with increased initiative and attentiveness. (**N,N**)

Report Card and IEP Comments 107

- _____ is **encouraged to listen** patiently to **opinions** of others **and wait for** his/her **turn to speak. Interrupting lessons** or other speakers by **making comments, getting out of seat**, and **speaking out of turn hinders learning for everyone. (N,N)**

- _____ **must listen patiently to opinions of others** and **wait for his/her turn to speak. Interrupting lessons by regularly getting out of seat, making noises**, and **speaking out of turn** continue to be a **serious hindrance** to learning for _____. **(N,N)**

- _____ often **speaks out of impulse, with a limited sense of when to speak and for how long. Habitual** (persistent/ frequent/ recurring/ periodic) **distractibility** and lack of focus (are a **major concern**) and **have often hindered** successful communication with teachers and peers. **(N,N)**

- _____ is an **enthusiastic participant** in a wide range of learning activities **but needs to learn to work on following teacher instructions. In spite of frequent reminders and requests,** _____ **'s lack of cooperation continues** to undermine the classroom learning environment. **(N,N)**

- _____ **continues to be distracted by minor events** around him/her during periods of oral instruction. He/she is **encouraged to be more consistent** with **starting assigned tasks** within a reasonable amount of time, and **following them through to completion without losing focus. (N,N)**

- _____ **works best** in a situation **with minimal distractions. When** he/she is **interested** in the topic at hand, he/she **can be focused** for short periods of time. _____ **requires teacher support and frequent reminders to remain on task, remain focused**, and **not interrupt the lesson. (N,N)**

- **Restlessness, complaining,** and **frequent verbal interruptions continue to interfere** with daily learning. _____ often **interrupts lessons without regard for others** or for the consequences. **Habitual** (persistent/ frequent/ recurring/ periodic) **distractibility** and **lack of focus continue to be a major concern. (N,N)**

- _____ **continues to have difficulty following** teacher **instructions** and (**very often**) **needs reminders to begin tasks** and **see them to completion.** _____ is often observed **wandering around the classroom, starting conversations during lessons**, and **interrupting** the learning of others. **(N,N)**

- _____ is **experiencing difficulty behaving** in an appropriate manner during class time, and is having **difficulty controlling** his/her **emotional outbursts**. Through teacher support and guidance, as well as a **social skills program**, it is hoped that _____ will soon experience improvement in this area. **(N,N)**

- **Restlessness, complaining,** and **habitual** (persistent/ frequent/ recurring/ periodic) **verbal interruptions** continue to **interfere with daily learning.** _____ often **interrupts lessons without regard for** others or for the consequences. **Frequent distractibility** and **lack of focus continue to be a concern.** _____ is **encouraged to focus** on tasks and **make an effort to complete** all **work** as instructed. **(N,N,N)**

Report Card and IEP Comments

Accepting Responsibility for Own Behavior

Positive

- _____ shows responsibility in **attendance**, **punctuality**, and **task completion**. (**P**)

- _____ is **showing increased willingness to focus** on and **complete assigned work** in class. (**P**)

- **Some progress was observed**, and _____ is **to be commended** for his/her **willingness** and **enthusiasm to succeed**. (**P**)

Positive/Negative

- _____ **continues to improve** in this area **but at a slower pace. Verbal interruptions** and **negativity** by _____ are hindering learning. (**P,N**)

- _____ is **learning the importance of taking responsibility for own learning**. With his/her participation in _____ and _____, _____ is beginning to recognize how his/her behavior can affect learning in a more positive way. _____ **needs to** continue to **work on** his/her **problem-solving skills** by learning how to resolve problems effectively (e.g., **taking responsibility** for the situation **instead of blaming others**). (**P,N**)

Negative

- _____ **needs to come** to each class **prepared with a (pencil, red pen, eraser,** and **ruler**). (**N**)

- _____ **needs to assume greater responsibility for demonstrating class behaviors** necessary for academic success. (**N**)

- **Inconsistency in attitude** and classroom **behavior** necessary for further growth **continue to hinder progress**. (**N,N**)

- _____ is an **enthusiastic participant** in a wide range of learning activities **but needs to learn to work on following teacher instructions. In spite of frequent reminders and requests,** _____ 's **lack of cooperation continues** to undermine the classroom learning environment. (**N,N**)

- _____ is **an active participant** in a wide range of learning activities but **needs to learn to work on listening to ideas of others, without interrupting. In spite of frequent reminders, requests,** and **parent communication,** _____ **'s lack of cooperation continues to undermine the classroom learning environment. (N,N)**

Report Card and IEP Comments

Class Behavior
Necessary for Academic Success

Positive

- _____ **shows ability to pay attention** in class. (**P**)

- _____ **listens** and **does not interrupt** the class **with off-topic comments**. (**P**)

- **With teacher assistance,** _____ **is learning how to conduct** himself/herself **appropriately** during class. (**P**)

- _____ **shows ability to pay attention** in class, **asking** and **appropriately answering** relevant **questions**. (**P**)

- **Some progress was observed**, and _____ is to be commended for his/her **willingness** and **enthusiasm to succeed**. (**P**)

- **Homework completion was more consistent this term**. _____ has also made **noticeable effort to improve** the **quality of work** done in class. (**P**)

- **Working independently** has been **much less** of **a concern** this term. Due to a **greater effort,** _____ has also **exhibited growth** in **areas** of **organizational skills, motivation,** and **following of instructions**. (**P**)

- _____ **is beginning to develop effective work habits**. He/she **usually perseveres with learning tasks** and **seeks help** from his/her peers or teacher. **Homework** is **usually completed on time**. He/she is reminded to **exercise care** in all his/her **work**. (**P**)

- _____ is **to be commended for requiring fewer reminders to remain focused** and **on task** in class. _____ has **assumed a greater responsibility for maintenance** and **use of school his/her organizer** and has **developed** a **more consistent homework routine**. (**P**)

Positive/Negative

- _____ **continues to improve** in this area **but at a slower pace. Verbal interruptions** and **negativity** by _____ are **hindering** learning. (**P,N**)

- _____ **participates actively** in our class **discussions** and **shares** a lot of **excellent ideas. Knowing** for **how long to speak** and **when to stop** would make interpersonal **communication** more meaningful and effective. _____ often **works on more than one task at a time**. Personal **work space, binder,** and **desk area require more thorough attention** and regular cleanup. (**P,N**)

- _____ often participates in class and is willing to answer questions and offer suggestions; however, limited ability to concentrate and stay on topic make clear communication difficult. _____ is encouraged to make a conscious effort to speak at a slower pace, focusing on clear and accurate enunciation of words. (P,N)

- _____ participates actively in our class discussions and shares a lot of excellent ideas. It is important that _____ make an effort to not verbally interrupt the lessons, as this impairs the learning of other students. _____ often works on more than one task at a time. Personal work space, binder, and desk area require more thorough attention and regular cleanup. (P,N)

- _____ still does not complete all of the assigned homework assignments, and this remains an area for improvement next year. He/she is to be congratulated for his/her increased effort to concentrate and produce better quality work in class. (N,P)

- _____ often follows oral instructions but continues to have some difficulty maintaining concentration and focus, especially if other distractions are present in the room. He/she is encouraged to make a conscious effort to ignore such distractions. When working in a small cooperative group setting, _____ always assists others who need help. (N,P)

Negative

- _____ is easily distracted from his/her work. (N)

- To achieve academic gains, this is an area that must improve. (N)

- _____ is encouraged to listen to teacher instructions during learning activities. (N)

- _____ requires assistance, support, and reminders to complete all assigned work. (N)

- Interrupting the lesson or other speakers takes away from the flow of classroom activities. (N)

- Less socializing and greater concentration would produce even better results in this course. (N)

- Inconsistent performance, effort, and focus upon learning have hindered academic growth this term. (N)

- Distractibility often (frequently) prevents successful and appropriate communication with teachers and peers. (N)

- Inconsistent performance, effort, and focus upon learning continue to seriously hinder academic growth. (N)

- Habitual (persistent/ frequent/ recurring/ periodic) distractibility and lack of focus continue to be/are a (serious) concern. (N)

Report Card and IEP Comments

- **Inability to remain focused** and **follow instructions** has had an **impact** on _____'s **academic progress**. (**N**)

- _____ needs to **assume greater responsibility for demonstrating class behaviors** conducive to academic success. (**N**)

- **Knowing for how long to speak** and **when to stop** would make interpersonal **communication** more meaningful and effective. (**N**)

- _____ is encouraged to **resist the temptation** to **vocalize displeasure** to the **entire class** when things don't turn out as expected. (**N**)

- **Distractibility** (*often frequently/ very often/ always/ regularly*) **prevents** successful and appropriate **communication** with teachers and peers. (**N**)

- _____ needs to **assume greater responsibility** for **being prepared** for class with **notes** and **materials readily available** to **commence work**. (**N**)

- _____ **needs frequent reminders not to interrupt** and **to work quietly. Greater degree of self-control** during lessons **must be exercised**. (**N**)

- _____ is **encouraged to participate in class and group activities** and **ask questions to clarify meaning** and **ensure understanding**. (**N**)

- Unfortunately, **very unpredictable classroom behavior** and **inconsistent completion of assignments** have made additional **progress extremely slow** and **difficult**. (**N**)

- _____ **must accept responsibility for recording of homework** and timely **completion of assigned tasks.** He/she must also **rely less on others** to do this task for him/her. (**N**)

- **Habitual** (persistent/ frequent/ recurring/ periodic) **distractibility** and **lack of focus** (*often/ very often/ usually*) **prevent** (hinder/ inhibit) successful **communication** with teachers and peers. (**N**)

- _____ **has difficulty adjusting to the routines** and **expectations** of the classroom. He/she **has difficulty cooperating** in **small groups** and **requires much assistance** when attempting **independent work**. (**N**)

- _____ is **encouraged to listen** and **consider ideas of others without interrupting** and **being negative. Frequent vocal complaints** and **negative comments** continue to undermine the classroom learning environment. (**N**)

- _____ **sometimes needs reminders to remain focused** and **on task. Following classroom routines** and **meeting behavioral expectations would help** _____ **attend** to the given task and **meet academic challenges** of our program **with more success**. (**N**)

- _____ **sometimes needs reminders to remain focused** and **on task.** Following **classroom routines** and **meeting** the **behavioral expectations would help** _____ attend to the task at hand and meet the academic challenges of our program with more success. (**N**)

- _____ **is experiencing some difficulty remaining on task, using class time wisely**, and **focusing** upon learning. In order for _____ to continue to learn, he/she **must ensure** that all **homework assignments** are **completed** and **submitted** for **evaluation on time**. **(N)**

- _____ was not able to demonstrate an understanding of the materials covered in class as he/she **did not begin** or **complete any** (most) **class assignments**. _____ **did not seek additional assistance although** this option **was offered** to him/her on a daily basis. **(N)**

- It is important that _____ make an **effort to not verbally interrupt** the lessons as this impairs the learning of other students. _____ **often works** on **more than one task** at a time. **Personal work space, binder,** and **desk area require more thorough attention** and **regular cleanup**. **(N)**

- **Greater degree** of **self-control** during lessons **must be exercised**. When confronted with **frustrating situations**, _____ is encouraged to deal with them by using the **practical problem-solving strategies** and the **stop, think method**. _____ will continue to receive assistance in this area. **(N)**

- _____ **requires assistance, support,** and **reminders to complete all assigned work**. _____ **is encouraged to make** a **greater effort** to **use** the **school organizer** as an organizational tool. **Inconsistent performance, effort,** and **focus** upon learning **have hindered academic growth** this term. **(N)**

- _____ **requires some assistance, support,** and **reminders to complete** all **assigned work**. _____ is **encouraged to make a greater effort in using the school organizer** as a tool that helps and reminds of homework, assignment, and test due dates. **Performance** in class **has been inconsistent** this term. **(N)**

- _____ **rarely completes and submits homework assignments. Numerous "homework not done" notes have been sent home** as a signal for **concern** in this area. **Learning strategies** on how to acquire and demonstrate specific class behaviors necessary for academic success have been, and **continue to be, shared** with _____. **(N)**

- _____ makes an effort but **often experiences difficulty conducting** himself/herself in an appropriate manner during class time. _____ **needs frequent reminders not to interrupt, remain focused,** and **on task**. Through teacher support and guidance, as well as a social skills program, it is hoped that _____ will soon experience improvement in this area. **(N)**

- _____ **needs reminders to remain focused,** and **on task,** and **not verbally interrupt the lessons**. _____ **must ensure that all homework tasks are completed** on time. It is recommended that _____ assume **greater responsibility for maintenance and effective use of school organizer**, and development of a **consistent homework routine**. **(N)**

- _____ **has been counseled on how to accept responsibility for behaviors** necessary for academic success. _____ is **reluctant to participate** in class

discussions and **reading** activities, and is **often content** with just **being** an **observer**. _____ is always encouraged to try his/her best and work to his/her full potential. **Inconsistent homework completion remains** a **concern** and a **hindrance** to learning. **(N)**

- _____ **needs to accept the consequences of** his/her **own choices. When faced** with a **conflict situation** with another student, _____ is usually **reluctant to see** a personal **role in the situation, preferring** to **place blame with** the **other individual.** He/she **needs to stop** and **think** before acting, in order to assess the consequences of his/her **choices.** A **behavior plan was developed** with _____ **to monitor** his/her **ability to make appropriate choices.** _____ **has not assumed responsibility for this plan** and thus has been unable to earn the rewards associated with good behavior. **(N)**

- **Inconsistency in attitude** and classroom **behavior** necessary for further growth **continue** to **hinder progress. (N,N)**

- **Demonstrating** a **sense** of **when to speak, when to listen,** and **how much to say remains a** (big/ huge/ serious) **challenge. (N,N)**

- _____ is encouraged to resist the temptation to **vocalize displeasure** to the entire class **when things don't turn out as expected. (N,N)**

- _____ still **needs reminders to remain focused** and **on task.** _____ **continues to arrive late to class on a regular basis,** especially in the afternoon. **(N,N)**

- _____ **continues to have difficulty focusing upon learning** and **needs reminders** to **remain on task** and **refrain from frequent lesson interruptions. (N,N)**

- **Arriving to class with required materials, focusing upon learning, completing assignments,** and **meeting** the **classroom expectations continue to be a challenge** for _____. **(N,N)**

- _____ often **speaks out of impulse, with a limited sense of when to speak** and **for how long. Frequent distractibility** and **lack of focus** (*are a **major concern**/ **have** often **hindered** successful **communication** with teachers and peers*). **(N,N)**

- _____ **often arrives** to class **without** his/her **homework.** He/she **requires constant reminders to finish** his/her **work** and **hand in assignments.** _____ **needs to use the school organizer on a daily basis** to monitor work that needs to be completed. **(N,N)**

- _____ is experiencing **difficulty behaving** appropriately and **controlling emotional outbursts** during class time. Through teacher support and guidance, as well as a social skills program, it is hoped that _____ will soon experience improvement in this area. **(N,N)**

- **Arriving to class with required materials, focusing upon learning, completing assignments, following classroom routines,** and **meeting the behavioral expectations** appear to be **a great challenge** for _____, in spite of the learning strategies that are already in place. **(N,N)**

- _____ is an **enthusiastic participant** in a wide range of learning activities **but needs to learn to work on following teacher instructions. In spite of frequent**

reminders and **requests,** _____ **'s lack of cooperation continues** to undermine the classroom learning environment. **(N,N)**

- _____ **continues to require reminders to remain focused** and **on task. Following classroom routines, refraining from interrupting,** and **meeting the behavioral expectations would help** _____ attend to the task at hand and meet the academic challenges of our program with even more success. **(N,N)**

- _____ is **an active participant** in a wide range of learning activities but **needs to learn to work** on **listening** to **ideas of others without interrupting. In spite of frequent reminders, requests,** and **parent communication,** _____ **'s lack of cooperation continues to undermine the classroom learning environment. (N,N)**

- _____ **inconsistently completes** and **submits homework** assignments. _____ **has not made effective use** of his/her **organizer** this term, and is encouraged to make improvements in this area. **Inconsistent performance, effort,** and **focus** upon learning are **hindering academic growth.** _____ **needs to follow teacher's instructions** and **improve** classroom **work habits. (N,N)**

- _____ **continues to experience difficulty behaving** in an appropriate manner during class time, and is **often having difficulty controlling** his/her **emotional** and **verbal outbursts.** _____ **needs frequent reminders to work quietly** and **not to interrupt.** Through **teacher support,** a **social skills program,** and **improvement in attitude,** it is hoped that _____ will experience success in this area. **(N,N)**

- _____ **continues to require assistance and support to complete all required homework** assignments. _____ is **encouraged to make a greater effort to use** the **school agenda** as an organizational tool. **Inconsistent performance, effort,** and **focus upon learning continue to seriously hinder academic growth. It is important** that _____ **make an effort not to verbally interrupt** the lessons, as this impairs the learning of other students. **(N,N)**

- _____ **continues to experience difficulty behaving** appropriately during class. _____ has been observed having **difficulty controlling frequent verbal interruptions.** _____ **needs regular reminders to remain focused, work quietly,** and **refrain from walking around** the classroom and striking up conversations with others. **Homework completion** and appropriate use of **organizer** remain a **concern.** Through **teacher support, parent contact,** and improved **attitude,** it is hoped that _____ will experience success in these areas. **(N,N)**

- _____ **still needs reminders to remain focused** and **on task. Following classroom routines, complaining less,** and **meeting the behavioral expectations would help** _____ attend to the task at hand and meet the academic challenges of our program with more success. _____ **must ensure** that all **homework tasks are completed** on time. It is recommended that _____ assume greater responsibility for maintenance and effective use of his/her **school organizer**, and development of a consistent **homework** routine. **(N,N)**

Report Card and IEP Comments

- _____ has been counseled on how to accept responsibility for his/her **behavior**. _____ **is extremely reluctant to acknowledge** his/her **part in classroom conflicts**. _____ **needs to practice this skill at home** in order **to be capable of social interaction** at the high school level. _____ **has received much advocacy** from his/her teachers at school, and he/she is always encouraged to try his/her best. **(N,N,N)**

- _____ **has difficulty adjusting to the routines and expectations** of the classroom. _____ **has difficulty cooperating in small groups** and **requires much assistance when attempting independent work**. _____ **demonstrates** an **eagerness to do well, yet does not always follow through** with commitment. He/she **has a tendency to distract** himself/herself and **needs to pay closer attention** in class, **use class time wisely,** and **focus** on his/her efforts rather than one those around him/her so that he/she may experience greater success. **(N,N,N)**

Self-Control

Positive

- _____ **demonstrates an ability to pay attention** in class. (**P**)

- _____ **listens** and **does not interrupt** the class **with off-the-topic comments**. (**P**)

- _____ is **showing increased willingness** to **focus** and **complete assigned work** in class. (**P**)

- **Some progress** was **observed**, and _____ is to be **commended** for his/her **determination** (desire) and **enthusiasm to succeed**. (**P**)

- **When in a structured environment**, _____ is **able to demonstrate a certain degree of self-control**. _____ will be encouraged and supported in his/her effort to improve in this area. (**P**)

- **Restlessness**, **complaining**, and **frequent verbal interruptions have reduced** in **number** and **frequency**. _____ is now **exercising** much **greater self-control** in class, making learning an easier and more rewarding task. (**P**)

- Toward the end of term one, _____ **began to make small gains in** his/her **ability to control behavior**. _____ is **having fewer emotional outbursts** during class, and is **able to interact more appropriately** with his/her peers. (**P**)

- _____ is **making** an **effort to improve self-control**, especially when he/she feels that there is something important to contribute to a class discussion, but finds it difficult to wait. With teacher assistance, he/she **is learning to recognize the frustration-producing situations** and **respond** to them **appropriately**. (**P**)

- _____ **has** the **ability** to **work constructively** in small and large **group settings**. He/she **continues to employ strategies to improve focus**. In addition, _____ is **starting to listen** and **take into consideration opposing** or different **opinions** of others in class. He/she is encouraged to remember to always stop and think before acting. (**P**)

Positive/Negative

- _____ **is making an effort to exercise self-control** in class. **When he/she is frustrated, this becomes a very difficult task** for him/her. (**P,N**)

- _____ **continues to improve** in this area **but at a slower pace. Verbal interruptions**, **complaining**, and **negativity** by _____ are hindering learning. (**P,N**)

- _____ **has made a greater effort in applying** the taught **problem-solving/ decision-making skills** in class this term. _____ **must make sure** that **only appropriate language** is **used** within a classroom setting. (**P,N**)

- **At times,** _____ is **able to listen attentively** to class discussions. _____ experiences **difficulty discerning when it is appropriate to voice** his/her **opinion** in class, **frequently disrupting** a lesson in progress. _____ **needs regular reminders to remain focused on the task** at hand in order to ensure a successful outcome. (**P,N**)

- _____ is **making an effort to exercise self-control** in class; **however, restlessness** and **frequent verbal interruptions** continue to be a hindrance to learning. **When is frustrated** he/she or overly **excited** it takes _____ a **long time to get settled** and **participate constructively** in class. (**P,N**)

- This is an **area of tangible growth** for _____. _____ is **able to listen attentively to class discussions** when he/she sets his/her mind to it. He/she **continues to experience some difficulty discerning when it is appropriate to voice** his/her **opinion** in class, but it is clear that he/she **understands that this hinders learning** and **disrupts** a lesson in progress. (**P,N**)

- _____ 's **self-control** is **inconsistent**. With teacher assistance, he/she **continues to learn to recognize the frustration-producing situations** and **respond** to them **appropriately**. _____ **needs to identify a problem situation** and then **consciously choose to use** the **stop, think, and act strategy before reacting emotionally**. (**N,P**)

Negative

- **Better concentration** in class would improve achievement in this and other areas. (**N**)

- _____ needs to develop **better problem-solving** and **decision-making skills**.(**N**)

- _____ 's **interrupting the lesson** or **other speakers** takes away from the flow of classroom activities. (**N**)

- _____ **often needs reminders** to **demonstrate appropriate problem-solving/ decision-making skills**. (**N**)

- **Habitual** (persistent/ frequent/ recurring/ periodic) **distractibility** and **lack of focus** (*continue to be/ are*) **a concern**. (**N**)

- **Inability to remain focused and follow instructions has had an impact on** _____ 's **academic progress**. (**N**)

- **Distractibility** often (frequently) **prevents successful and appropriate communication** with teachers and peers. (**N**)

- _____ has **difficulty cooperating in small groups** and **requires much assistance** when asked to do **independent work**. (**N**)

- _____ is **encouraged to resist** the **temptation** to **vocalize displeasure** to the **entire class** when things don't turn out as expected. (**N**)

- **Habitual** (persistent/ frequent/ recurring/ periodic) **distractibility** and **lack of focus** often prevent (hinder/ inhibit) **successful communication** with teachers and peers. (**N**)

- _____ at times still uses **inappropriate language** in class. He/she **needs to be reminded** to **demonstrate appropriate problem-solving/ decision-making skills** on a daily basis. (**N**)

- _____ continues to **need reminders to make reliable decisions**. He/she **still needs to remember to reflect**, **think**, and then try to **solve problems** with **input** from peers and teachers. (**N**)

- _____ **sometimes applies** the **learned problem-solving/ decision-making skills** in class. **There are times when** it appears that _____ makes a **conscious decision not to exercise self-control** during class. (**N**)

- _____ is a **cheerful student**. However, he/she **often does not use appropriate language during discussion** or **when addressing peers**. _____ is encouraged to **stop** and **think before speaking** and **verbally interrupting**. (**N**)

- **Greater degree** of **self-control during lessons must be exercised. When confronted with frustrating situations,** _____ is encouraged to deal with them by using the practical **problem-solving strategies** such as the **stop, think method.** _____ will continue to receive assistance in this area. (**N**)

- _____ **has difficulty remaining in** his/her **seat** during independent work periods. As he/she **wanders** the classroom, _____ **often distracts others** from learning and does not accomplish his/her own work. _____ **needs to be reminded that permission is needed to leave his/her seat** during a lesson. (**N**)

- _____ **needs to follow school and classroom rules** and **routines.** _____ **needs to exercise self-control** and **calm down** in situations that are **frustrating** for him/ her to deal with. A **cool-down period is sometimes needed** to help _____ have a **better understanding of a situation**, and then **make good choices.** (**N**)

- _____ **often acts impulsively**, especially **during** class **discussions.** _____ **benefits from visual cues** and **verbal reminders to keep focused** and **take turns** during group discussions. _____ is **rewarded computer time** when assigned tasks are completed. **Praise** and **encouragement help** _____ feel more confident in a **group learning situation.** (**N**)

- **Habitual** (persistent/ frequent/ recurring/ periodic) **distractibility** and **lack of focus** are (serious) **concerns. (N,N)**

- **Demonstrating** a **sense of when to speak**, **when to listen**, and **how much to say** remains a **challenge. (N,N)**

- **Inconsistency in attitude** and classroom **behavior** necessary for further growth continue to **hinder progress. (N,N)**

Report Card and IEP Comments

- ._____ is encouraged to **show respect** for the **learning environment** of peers by **refraining from continuous verbal interruptions**. (N,N)

- _____ is encouraged to **resist** the **temptation to vocalize displeasure** to the entire class, especially **when things don't turn out as expected**. (N,N)

- **Restlessness, complaining,** and **frequent verbal interruptions continue** to be a hindrance to learning. **Greater self-control must be exercised** if measurable academic growth is to occur. **(N,N)**

- _____ tends to **speak out in class, rather than raise** his/her **hand**. He/she **requires frequent reminders to remain on task** and **works best** with **direct teacher support** and **intervention**. (N,N)

- _____ has a **tendency to distract** himself/herself and **needs to pay closer attention** in class, **use class time wisely**, and **focus** on his/her efforts, **rather than those around** him/her. To experience greater success this will need to change. **(N,N)**

- _____ is an **enthusiastic participant** in a wide range of learning activities **but needs to learn to work** on **following teacher instructions. In spite** of **frequent reminders** and **requests,** _____'s **lack of cooperation continues** to **undermine** the classroom learning environment. **(N,N)**

- _____ **is experiencing difficulty behaving in an appropriate manner** during class, and **has difficulty controlling emotional outbursts**. Through teacher support and guidance, as well as social skills program, it is hoped that _____ will soon experience improvement in this area. **(N,N)**

- **Greater degree of self-control** during lessons **is expected**. _____ is encouraged to **show respect** for the **learning environment** of peers by **refraining from continuous verbal interruptions. Following** classroom **routines** and **meeting** the classroom **behavior expectations must take place** if _____ is to experience progress in learning. **(N,N)**

- This is an area of **tangible growth** for _____. He/she **is able to listen** attentively to class discussions **when** he/she **sets** his/her **mind to it**. He/she **continues to experience some difficulty discerning when it is appropriate to voice** his/her **opinion** in class. **Close observations** appear to **show** that _____ **understands that this hinders learning** and **disrupts lessons in progress**. **(N,N)**

- _____ has **difficulty adjusting to the routines and expectations of the classroom**. _____ has **difficulty cooperating in small groups** and **requires much assistance** in order to do **independent work**. _____ **demonstrates an eagerness to do well, yet does not** always **follow through with commitment**. He/she has a **tendency to distract** himself/herself and must make an effort to **pay closer attention in class, use class time wisely,** and **focus** on personal efforts **rather than those of others around** him/her. **(N,N)**

- _____ often **speaks out of impulse, with a limited sense of when to speak and for how long. Frequent distractibility** and lack of focus (are **major concerns/ have often** *hindered* successful *communication* with teachers and peers). **(N,N,N)**

Report Card and IEP Comments

Effort and Motivation

Positive

- _____ 's **work often exhibits thought** and **care**. (**P**)

- _____ **has shown considerable improvement** in **effort** and **motivation** this term. (**P**)

- _____ **shows responsibility** in **attendance**, **punctuality**, and **task completion**. (**P**)

- **Much improved positive work habits** and **attitudes** are beginning to make a difference in achievement and learning this term. (**P**)

- **Some progress was observed**, and _____ is to be commended for his/her **determination** and **enthusiasm to succeed**. (**P**)

Positive/Negative

- _____ **continues to improve** in this area **but at a slower pace. Verbal interruptions** and **negativity** by _____ are **hindering** learning. (**P,N**)

- Since the last parent/teacher/student conference, and as a result of mutually agreed-upon strategies, **some improvement in effort** has been observed. _____, **however, must ensure that all assignments** are **handed in completed, on time, detailed,** and of **good quality**, for improved and observable academic growth to occur. (**P,N**)

Negative

- **To progress academically**, this is an area that **must improve**. (**N**)

- **To achieve** academic **progress**, this is an area that (must/ needs to) **improve**. (**N**)

- _____ **needs to come** to each class **pepared with** (a **pencil**, **red pen**, **eraser**, and **ruler**). (**N**)

- To fully achieve academic potential, assigned **tasks must be completed to the best of ability**. (**N**)

- **Distractibility** (*sometimes/ often/ frequently*) **prevents** successful and **appropriate communication** with teachers and peers. (**N**)

- When things don't turn out as expected, _____ is **encouraged to resist the temptation to vocalize displeasure** to the **entire class**. (**N**)

- He/she needs to **assume greater responsibility** for being **prepared** for class with **notes** and **materials readily available** to commence work. (**N**)

- If _____ is to fully achieve his/her academic potential, **assigned tasks** need to be **completed to the best of ability**, instead of being **satisfied with** the **very minimum**. (**N**)

- _____ was not able to demonstrate an understanding of the materials covered in class as he/she **did not begin**, or **complete**, **any** (most) **class assignments**. _____ **did not seek additional assistance although this option was offered** to him/her on a daily basis. (**N**)

- _____ **continues to need assignments that are modified**, both in **time** and **quantity. Assistance is necessary** in order for _____ **to complete** his/her work. He/she **still needs** frequent **reminders to stay on task. Home communication** has **helped** _____ **in the completion of assignments**, to some extent. (**N**)

- **Inconsistency in attitude** and classroom **behavior** necessary for further growth **continue to hinder progress**. (**N,N**)

- _____ 's **attitude, motivation,** and **enthusiasm** toward learning are still not at a level that would help him/her improve academic achievement. **Effort, motivation,** and **concentration** in class are **inconsistent**. (**N,N**)

- **Very little effort** and **motivation** are **evident** in spite of the learning strategies that are in place. _____ has **at times been observed telling other students not to do their best. Lack of effort** and **motivation** in school are a (serious) **concern**. (**N,N**)

- _____ is an **enthusiastic participant** in a wide range of learning activities **but needs to learn to work on following teacher instructions. In spite of** frequent **reminders and requests,** _____'s **lack of cooperation continues** to **undermine** the classroom learning environment. (**N,N**)

- _____ continues to **require** teacher **assistance in ensuring acceptable** and effective **organization** of **personal desk space, equipment, three-ring binder,** and **school organizer**/planner. _____ **must make** a **commitment** and **effort** in this area so that these things are done independently and without daily reminders. **Without a serious commitment, organizational skills** are not likely to improve. (**N,N**)

Positive Self-Image

Positive

- _____ **continues to develop confidence in class** and **new situations**. He/she has **put forth** a **significant effort this term, handing** in **assignments on time, volunteering answers,** and **participating in problem-solving activities**. _____ has been a **pace-setter** (great example) for his/her classmates. **(P,P)**

- _____ is **becoming more self-confident in social situations** both in class and elsewhere in the school. **(P)**

- _____ **interacts with** his/her **peers** during unstructured learning times **with more confidence,** and **without encouragement**. He/she **contributes ideas** in a **small class setting when** he/she feels that his/her opinion **needs to be heard**. **(P)**

- _____ continues to show an **increased interest** in **tackling academic challenges**. His/her **success in taking risks has positively increased** his/her **image** as a student. With continued risk taking, _____'s confidence is expected to increase. **(P)**

- _____ **is making some effort to participate** in class activities and group situations and **continues to develop confidence as a learner**. _____ is **encouraged to socialize more with** his/her **classmates** and **initiate conversations** with others. **(P)**

Positive/Negative

- _____ is making **some effort to participate in class** activities and group situations and **continues to develop confidence** as a learner. _____ is encouraged to **socialize more** with his/her classmates **and initiate conversations**. **(P,N)**

- _____ has **started to demonstrate** an **ability to accept constructive criticism** and **use it to improve** his/her **work. However, more consistent effort** in school work **is still required**. _____ **must take** his/her **time with all assignments**, and **review** and **edit** written **work. (P,N)**

- _____ is **beginning to recognize** his/her **own strengths** and **accomplishments**. He/she **usually initiates asking for assistance** when this is required. He/she is **encouraged to become more involved** in **school activities** and **take advantage of learning opportunities** by participating in _____. **(P,N)**

- **With increased success in completing assignments,** _____ has been **able to experience positive feedback** from peers and teachers. **To maintain a more positive self-image,** _____ **needs to become more consistent in completing** his/her **work to the best of ability**. In order to increase the likelihood of success, **personal strengths need to be maximized. (P,N)**

Negative

- _____ **participates infrequently** in class **activities** and **discussions**. He/she is **unfocused** during small group discussions, **often knowingly discussing subjects unrelated** to the assignment. He/she **resists suggestions to get back on task**. Next term, _____ is encouraged to take an **active role** in class **discussion**, as it will help him/her remain **focused** and become **productive**. (**N,N**)

- _____'s **attitude**, **motivation,** and **enthusiasm** for learning are **not at a level** that is required for further academic growth and improved level of achievement. _____ **often needs reminders to begin** his/her **work** and see even the simplest of academic **tasks** through to **completion**. In order to improve marks next term, a (much) **higher degree of effort is needed** and encouraged. (**N,N**)

Work Habits and Attitude

Positive

- **Much improved positive work habits** and **attitudes** are **beginning to make** a **difference in** _____'s **achievement and learning** this term. **(P)**

- _____'s **work often exhibits thought** and **care**. **(P)**

- _____ **shows interest** and **enthusiasm in** the **classroom**. **(P)**

- _____ **listens** and **does not interrupt** the class with **off**-the-**topic comments**. **(P)**

- _____ **shows responsibility** in **attendance**, **punctuality**, and **task completion**. **(P)**

- He/she has **demonstrated** a **positive attitude toward learning** and shown **good leadership skills**. **(P)**

- **Some progress was observed**, and _____ is to be commended for his/her **willingness** and **enthusiasm to succeed**. **(P)**

- _____ **demonstrates** an **ability to pay attention** in class, **asking** and **appropriately answering** relevant **questions**. **(P)**

Positive/Negative

- _____ **continues to improve** in this area, **but at a slower pace. Verbal interruptions** and **negativity** by _____ are hindering learning. **(P,N)**

- _____ is **showing** some **evidence** of **striving to improve independent work skills**. **Organizational skills, following instructions,** and **showing a more consistent motivation** (attitude) in class remain **areas for further improvement**. **(P,N)**

- _____ **is making** some **effort to participate** in class **activities** and **group situations** and **continues** to **develop confidence** as a learner. _____ is **encouraged to socialize more** with his/her classmates and **initiate conversations**. **(P,N)**

Negative

- _____ often **comes to class without** the **necessary equipment**. **(N)**

- All **school equipment must be brought to class daily**, ready for use and in working condition. (**N**)

- _____ **needs to come** to each class **prepared with** (a **pencil**, **red pen**, **eraser,** and **ruler**). (**N**)

- **Interrupting the lesson** or **other speakers** takes away from learning and the flow of classroom activities. (**N**)

- **Less socializing** and **greater concentration** would **produce** even **greater results** in this (*course/subject*). (**N**)

- **Distractibility** often (frequently) **prevents successful** and **appropriate communication** with teachers and peers. (**N**)

- **Most assignments** are **completed without adequate effort** and **many are not submitted** for **evaluation on time**. (**N**)

- _____ **continues to need significant assistance** in the **planning** and **completion of** his/her **assignments**. (**N**)

- **Frequent distractibility** and **lack of focus** often prevent (hinder/ inhibit) successful **communication** with teachers and peers. (**N**)

- _____ **needs reminders** to **use** his/her **organizer** and seek **frequent one-to-one assistance** in **order to complete** assigned **work**. (**N**)

- _____ needs to **assume greater responsibility** for **being prepared** for class with notes and **materials** readily available to commence work. (**N**)

- _____ **needs to assume greater responsibility** for **establishing** and **maintaining** an **effective study/homework routine** next year. (**N**)

- _____ has a **tendency to distract** himself/herself and **needs to pay closer attention** in class, **use class time wisely**, and **focus** on **personal effort** instead of activities of peers around him/her. (**N**)

- _____ continues to need **assignments modified** both **in time** and **quantity**. **Assistance is necessary** in order for _____ **to complete** his/her **work**. He/she **still needs** frequent **reminders** to **stay on task**. **Home communication** has helped. (**N**)

- _____ **is being taught appropriate work habits** in class. These include **finding** a **quiet spot for work, minimizing distractions, avoiding off-task behavior**, and **asking** for **assistance** when required. We will continue to monitor _____'s progress in this area. (**N**)

- _____ is encouraged to **resist temptations to vocalize displeasure** to the **entire class** when things don't turn out as expected. (**N**)

- **Frequent distractibility** and **lack of focus** are a (very serious) **concern**. (**N,N**)

- **Inconsistency in attitude** and classroom **behavior** necessary for further growth **continue** to **hinder progress. (N,N)**

- _____ is **encouraged to resist** the **temptation to vocalize displeasure** aloud **when things don't turn out as expected. (N,N)**

- _____ often **speaks out of impulse**, with a **limited sense of when to speak** and **for how long. Frequent distractibility** and lack of focus (are *major concerns/ have often hindered* successful *communication* with teachers and peers). **(N,N)**

- _____ is **encouraged to listen** and **consider ideas of others, without interrupting** and **being negative. Frequent vocal complaints** and **negative comments** are seriously **undermining** the classroom learning environment. **(N,N)**

- _____ is **an active participant** in a wide range of learning activities but **needs to learn** to **work** on **listening** to **ideas of others, without interrupting. In spite of frequent reminders, requests,** and **parent communication,** _____'s **lack of cooperation continues** to **undermine our** classroom **learning environment. (N,N)**

- _____ **has difficulty adjusting to the routines and expectations** of the classroom. He/she **has difficulty cooperating** in small groups and **requires much assistance when attempting independent work.** _____ **demonstrates** an **eagerness to do well, yet** does **not** always **follow through with commitment.** He/she **has** a **tendency to distract** himself/herself and **needs to pay closer attention** in class, **use class time wisely,** and **focus** more on personal efforts instead of those of other students around him/her. **(N,N)**

Report Card and IEP Comments

Organizational Skills

Positive

- Some **progress was observed**, and _____ is **to be commended** for his/her **willingness** and **enthusiasm to succeed**. **(P)**

- _____ is sometimes **able to prioritize** and **plan**. The use of a **time line** has **helped** _____ to visualize main steps in completion of assignments. He/she **is beginning to take more responsibility** for his/her success. **(P)**

- _____ has made **measurable** (tangible) **progress** in his/her attempt **to improve organizational skills**. **Almost all** of the **assigned work** has been **completed on time** and **with diligent care** and **effort** this term. **Congratulations** on your effort! **(P)**

- _____ **continues to make positive gains** in the _____ program, namely in the area of **organizational skills**. _____ **now listens** to **teacher advice** and **suggestions** and is **making** an **effort to become** a **better organized student**. **(P)**

- _____ is usually **able** to **complete** most of his/her **daily required assignments** in class. He/she **has learned to organize** his/her **time effectively** and **completes one task before** starting another. _____ is **able** to **complete successfully all given work** with **minimal teacher reminders**. **Homework assignments have** also **been adhered to**. **(P)**

- _____ has **progressed impressively** in his/her **attempt to improve organizational skills**. Almost all of the assigned work has been completed on time and with **diligent care** and **effort**. _____ is **able to plan** and **set personal academic** and **nonacademic goals independently** and with very little teacher assistance. **Congratulations** on doing well in this area! **(P)**

Positive/Negative

- _____ has made **some effort** in **completing homework**, assigned **tasks**, and **returning materials**. A **more consistent** and **independent use** of our **school organizer** is **highly recommended**. **(P,N)**

- **With constant support**, _____ is **learning to organize** his/her materials and work in a consistent manner. _____ **needs to be reminded to bring** the **necessary items to class** on a daily basis (every day). **(P,N)**

- **Although equipment** and **materials** are **usually brought to class**, _____ **occasionally** does **not meet** assignment **deadlines**. He/she **will need to continue** to **work on making reference to** the school **organizer** on a daily basis. **(P,N)**

- _____ **usually arrives to class with appropriate materials**. When necessary, he/she is **usually able to locate** the **necessary notes** in his/her binder. _____

Copyright © 2001, 2003, 2009 by Stevan Krajnjan

(*sometimes/ usually/ occasionally*) has **difficulty** with **task completion. Homework is often incomplete** and **assignments** are **not handed in on time**. _____ (*sometimes/ usually/ occasionally*) **requires direct teacher intervention** in order **to start** and **complete tasks**. (**P,N**)

- **With regular** teacher **support** and **reminders,** _____ is **learning to organize** his/her **materials and personal desk space.** _____ **needs to recognize** the **importance of possessing** good **organizational skills** for academic success now and in the years to come. _____ **must use** his/her **school organizer more effectively** to ensure that assignments and other activities are completed on time. (**P,N**)

- During the latter part of this term, _____ has **shown some improvement** in **completing** and **submitting** his/her **assignments** on the dates they were due. **However, there** is **often a long time delay between taking out materials** and **starting to listening** and **following the lesson. This causes** him/her to **lag behind.** _____ is **encouraged to be prepared** with **materials** within a reasonable time frame, especially by the start of the lesson. (**P,N**)

- A **daily planner** and **oral reminders** are **used to help** _____ improve upon his/her **organizational skills.** With encouragement, _____ is learning to use his/her **planner** to help him/her complete assignments on time. (**N,P**)

Negative

- _____ frequently **comes to class without** the **necessary equipment.** (**N**)

- _____ **requires direct teacher intervention** in order **to start** and **complete tasks.** (**N**)

- _____ **needs to come** to each class **prepared with** (a **pencil**, **red pen**, **eraser,** and **ruler**). (**N**)

- **Personal desk space, binders,** and other **school equipment require better** and **more thorough organization.** (**N**)

- All **school equipment must be brought to class, ready for use,** and **in working condition** on **daily** basis. (**N**)

- _____ **needs reminders to use** his/her **planner** and **requires frequent one-to-one assistance** in order **to complete** his/her **work.** (**N**)

- _____ continues to **require teacher assistance** and regular **reminders to organize materials** and **personal desk space.** (**N**)

- _____ needs to **assume greater responsibility for being prepared** for class with **notes** and **materials** readily available to commence (begin/ start) work. (**N**)

- _____ **must accept responsibility for recording homework** and **long-term** assignments **in** his/her **organizer** and **for completing tasks on time** (by due date). (**N**)

- _____ has **made** some **effort in completing homework and assigned tasks**, and in **returning materials**. A **more consistent** and **independent use** of our school organizer **is highly recommended**. (**N**)

- **Bringing needed supplies** to class, and **having notes properly placed in a binder** according to subject, are **organizational skills** that _____ will require continued support, on daily basis (every day). (**N**)

- _____ continues to **need assistance to organize personal desk space**, **binders**, and other **school equipment**. _____ **receives regular reminders** and **tips** on how to improve organizational skills. (**N**)

- _____ **requires frequent reminders to begin tasks** and **remain focused**. He/she is **encouraged to listen to all instructions**, and **ask questions to clarify information** he/she does not understand. (**N**)

- _____ **continues to need** assistance **to organize** his/her **work** and **assignments**. He/she **often needs reminders to focus** on the work at hand. _____ has **difficulty sustaining** a **consistent** work **effort**. (**N**)

- _____ **needs gentle** (regular/ frequent/ daily) **reminders to keep** his/her **school binder, desk**, and **personal work place** well **organized. With** teacher **assistance**, _____ **continues to develop** his/her **organizational skills**. (**N**)

- **Personal desk, space, binders**, and other **school equipment require improved** and **more thorough organization**. A **more consistent effort** in **completing homework** assignments **is required. Some work is not completed on time**. (**N**)

- _____ continues to experience **difficulty in keeping** himself/herself **organized** this term. He/she **frequently comes to class without** the **required materials**. Increased **effort to catch up on assignments missed** due to absence **is required**. (**N**)

- _____ **has had some difficulty this term meeting the time lines** for his/her assignments. He/she **needs to make reference to** his/her school **organizer on a regular basis**, and **budget** personal **time** in order to complete and submit work on time. (**N**)

- **With regular teacher support** and **reminders**, _____ **is learning to organize** his/her **materials** and **personal desk** space. _____ has **not made an effort to organize loose sheets** and **handouts** in his/her binder **in spite of regular reminders** and **teacher assistance**. (**N**)

- _____ is encouraged to **spend** a bit **more time each day examining** the **condition of** his/her **desk, school binder**, and **personal school equipment. In spite of regular reminders** and other teaching strategies being in place, development of **organizational skills continues** to be an **area of need** (for _____). (**N**)

- _____ has **often come to class** this term **without proper notebooks** and **written work**. They remain either in his/her locker or at home. He/she is **encouraged to spend more time making sure that** he/she **checks** his/her **agenda** and **is**

prepared the day before with all assignments and **materials** necessary to make learning successful. **(N)**

- _____ is **encouraged to use** his/her **school agenda as a tool** to help keep himself/herself organized on a daily basis. _____ **frequently arrives to class without materials**, which **hinders** his/her ability to **initiate** assigned tasks. A **posted timetable** and **back-up supplies** of pencils, paper, etc. have helped _____ **to regain** his/her **focus** and plan his/her day. **(N)**

- _____ continues to **require** teacher **assistance in ensuring acceptable** and **effective use of personal desk space, equipment, three-ring binder**, and **school organizer/planner**. _____ **must make** a **commitment** and **effort** in this area so that these tasks are done independently, and without daily reminders. **Without a serious commitment**, organizational skills are **unlikely to improve**. **(N)**

- _____ **requires frequent reminders** and **assistance to keep** his/her **own personal work space tidy** and **organized**. _____ is, again, **reminded to recognize the importance** of possessing **good organizational skills** for academic success. _____ **must make** a **conscious effort to use** his/her **organizer more effectively** and **ensure** that **assignments** and other activities are **completed on time**. **(N)**

- _____ **requires reminders to keep** his/her **own personal work space tidy** and **organized**. _____ is **guided to use** an **eraser** or **score through the word when an error is made, rather** than **scratching** or **writing over letters**. He/she **often squeezes** his/her **sentences into one line rather than spacing them out**, thereby leaving no spaces between words or making his/her work illegible. He/she is **reminded to come to class with** (a **highlighter** and a **calculator**). **(N)**

- _____ has **experienced difficulty** with the **proper organization** of his/her **notebooks** and **materials**. He/she **needs to refer to** his/her **school agenda to ensure that all assignments** are **completed** with **effort by the due dates**. In addition, all **papers need to be placed in their proper location** at the moment they are given, **in** the **correct** subject **notebook**. **(N)**

- _____ **continues to ignore suggestions** aimed at improving **organizational skills**. **(N,N)**

- _____ has often **neglected to bring completed work to class** as it is often **forgotten** in the locker **or left at home**. He/she **needs to continue working** on **making** daily **regular reference to** the school **agenda** so that he/she can be better **prepared** for class. **(N,N)**

- **Very little effort** was made by _____ to **organize personal desk space, binder,** and **other school equipment**. _____ **received regular reminders** and **tips** on **how** to improve organizational skills, **most of which** he/she **chose not to put into practice**. **(N,N)**

- **In spite of regular reminders** and **close monitoring**, _____ (very) **often comes to class without** his/her **school organizer** and other **school equipment**. This has **seriously hindered learning** and **academic progress**. _____ **must become more responsible** for **arriving** to **class prepared** and **being ready to learn**. **(N,N)**

- _____ **requires frequent reminders and assistance to keep** his/her **own personal work space tidy** and **organized**. _____ is, again, reminded that he/she **needs to recognize** the **importance** of **possessing** good **organizational skills** for academic success now and in the years to come. _____ **must make** a **conscious effort to use** the school **organizer more effectively** to **ensure that assignments** and **other activities** are **completed on time**. **(N,N)**v

Sense of Ownership & Responsibility for Own Education

General

- **Work output**, **quality** of **assignments**, and **attitude** toward school achievement (*continue to improve/ remain consistent/ remain inconsistent/ have not improved in spite of intense teacher support, guidance, and assistance*). (**G**)

Positive

- _____ is **to be congratulated** for a **consistent effort** and **positive results** in this area. _____ **always works with diligence** in class, **volunteers** to **read**, and **completes** his/her **work to the best of ability. Much improved positive work habits** and **attitudes make it possible for** this **area of need** to be **taken off** the _____ term **IEP**. (**P,P**)

- **Some progress was observed**, and _____ is **to be commended** for his/her **willingness** and **enthusiasm to succeed.** (**P**)

- **Work output, effort, quality** of **assignments**, and **attitude** toward school **have been consistent**. This is **no longer** an **area of need.** (**P**)

- **Change in interest** and **enthusiasm about learning** have **improved academic achievement** this term. Keep up the effort, _____! (**P**)

- **Work output, quality** of **assignments**, and **attitude toward** school performance **continue** to **improve. Change** in **interest** and **enthusiasm about learning** have **improved** academic **achievement** this term. Keep up the effort, _____! (**P**)

- **Work output, quality** of **assignments,** *and* attitude toward school achievement **remain consistent. Publishing** of school work on the **computer** has **worked well** for _____. _____ is encouraged to continue to use the **computer** as a **publishing** and **word processing tool.** (**P**)

Positive/Negative

- _____ **has shown** a **willingness** to **accept** some **assistance** with school work, **but needs** to **assume** a **greater responsibility** for **own learning** and **independent** work. (**P,N**)

- _____ continues to **improve** in this area **but** at a **slower pace. Verbal interruptions** and **negativity** by _____ are hindering (continue to hinder) learning. (**P,N**)

- _____ demonstrates an **eagerness** to **do well, yet does not** always **follow through** with **commitment**. He/she has a **tendency** to **distract** himself/herself and **needs** to **pay closer attention** in **class**, use **class time wisely**, and **focus** on his/her **effort** rather than on those around him/her, so that he/she may experience greater **success**. **(P,N)**

- _____ has been **willing** to **try tasks** that have been highly structured. **However,** he/she still **lacks confidence** and **motivation when faced** with **long-term assignments requiring** a **series of steps** before they are completed. He/she needs to **work** on **being more consistent** in terms of **following** long-term **projects through to completion**. **(P,N)**

- During this term, _____ **has begun** to **accept some responsibility for** his/her **learning. However,** there are times when he/she is **reluctant** to **commence** and **follow through** with **assigned tasks**. He/she needs to understand that, with assistance, he/she is **capable** of **completing work** that may initially appear overwhelming. This may help build his/her **self-confidence** and **self-esteem**. **(P,N)**

- **Completion** of **assignments** has been **more consistent** this term. _____ **works with** a **great deal of effort** on **projects** and assignments **that are of interest. Consistency in effort are required in all areas** of the curriculum. _____ **has the ability to work independently and in groups** with others where he/she often **assumes a position of leadership**. **(P,N)**

- **Inconsistent homework completion remains** a **serious concern** and a **hindrance** to learning. _____ **needs to assume greater responsibility** for **establishing** and **maintaining** an **effective study/homework routine** (next year/ next term). An **increase** in **effort on in-class tasks** was **observed** in the latter part of the (third) term. **(N,P)**

Negative

- _____ continues to **ignore suggestions** aimed at **improving organizational skills**. **(N)**

- **Interrupting lessons,** or **other speakers,** takes away from the **flow** of classroom activities. **(N)**

- He/she **needs to assume greater responsibility** for **being prepared** for class **with** notes and **materials readily available** to commence work. **(N)**

- _____ **needs** to **become** more **responsible** for his/her own education **by setting** a **clear goal** in (this area) and then **making sure** that **it is accomplished**. **(N)**

- **Work output, quality** of **assignments,** and **attitude** toward school performance **remain inconsistent**. _____'s **progress** is **being limited** by **lack of effort** to commence (begin) some assignments, or by **not following** them **through to completion**. **(N)**

- **Work output, quality of assignments,** and **attitude** toward school performance **are inconsistent**. _____'s **interest** and **enthusiasm about learning** seem to **fluctuate from day to day**. To improve, greater responsibility for own learning and independent work is encouraged. **(N)**

- **Timely completion of homework** and **daily** recording of homework in the organizer **must be in place** if _____'s learning is to continue to improve. **Thank you,** _____, for **making** a **deliberate effort** (during the latter part of this term) **to assume** more **responsibility for** your **own learning!** (N)

- _____ **needs to focus more on** his/her **studies** and **less on** his/her **peers** in order **to meet deadlines** and **produce quality assignments.** During class, he/she **is** frequently **off task.** These **off-task** tendencies **make it difficult** for _____ **to access** the **assistance** needed in order to **complete assignments.** He/she **completes tasks quickly,** after much **procrastination.** _____ is **encouraged to seek assistance** when necessary and work with his/her teachers to set short-term goals. (N)

- **Inconsistency in attitude** and classroom **behavior** necessary for further growth continue to **hinder progress.** (N,N)

- **Assignments** are **often incomplete, submitted late** for marking, or **not handed in at all.** _____ is encouraged to **work independently** in class. (N,N)

- _____ **has difficulty adjusting to** the **routines** and **expectations** of the classroom. He/she **finds it hard to cooperate** in **small groups,** and **requires much assistance** with independent work. (N,N)

- _____ continues to **ignore suggestions** aimed at **improving organizational skills. Work output, quality** of assignments, and **attitude** toward school performance **remain inconsistent.** _____'s **interest** and **enthusiasm** in learning **fluctuate** from day to day. To improve, **better attitude** and **following of teacher** instructions are strongly (very much/ highly) encouraged. (N,N)

Report Card and IEP Comments

Social Skills

Positive

- _____ **continues to make gains** in area of social skills. In addition to participating in (first term) extracurricular activities, he/she has **joined** the _____ **club** where he/she often assists with _____ and _____. _____ is **to be congratulated** on **positive interaction** with his/her peers and his/her **willingness to assist** those in need! **(P,P)**

- _____ **continues to make gains** in the area of social skills. **(P)**

- _____ **listens** and **does not interrupt** the class **with off-topic comments**. **(P)**

- _____ continues to have a **good** working **relationship** with other students in class. **(P)**

- _____ is becoming **more self-confident** in social situations both in class and elsewhere in the school. **(P)**

- **Some progress was observed**, and _____ is to be commended for his/her **willingness and enthusiasm to succeed**. **(P)**

- _____ **interacts with** his/her **peers** during unstructured learning times with **more confidence** and **without encouragement**. He/she **contributes ideas in a small class setting when** he/she feels that his/her opinion **needs to be heard**. **(P)**

Positive/Negative

- _____ continues to **improve** in this area **but at** a **slower pace. Verbal interruptions** and **negativity** (by _____) are hindering learning. **(P,N)**

- _____ **has been making** an **effort to respect** the **personal space** of others. He/she **needs reminders to attend to** his/her **work** during class time, **rather than becoming involved** in the negative **behavior** and **conversations** of other students. **(P,N)**

- _____ **often participates in class** and is **willing to answer questions** and **offer suggestions**; however, **limited ability to concentrate and stay on topic makes clear communication difficult**. _____ is **encouraged to make a conscious effort to speak at a slower** pace, focusing on **clear and accurate enunciation** of words. **(P,N)**

- _____ **continues to struggle with appropriate social skills** in class. _____ **is eager to interact with other students**, although it is **not always at an acceptable time**. _____ **is learning to interpret body language to aid** in him/her **knowing when it is acceptable to approach another person**. He/she **is also learning to refrain from speaking negatively about** his/her **peers** (others). **(N,P)**

Negative

- _____ **applies** the **learned social skills** and **strategies** in class **inconsistently**. (**N**)

- _____ 's **interrupting** the **lesson** or other speakers **takes away from** the **flow** of classroom activities. (**N**)

- **Distractibility** often (frequently) **prevents** successful and appropriate **communication** with teachers and peers. (**N**)

- **Frequent distractibility** and **lack of focus** often **prevent** (hinder/ inhibit) successful **communication** with teachers and peers. (**N**)

- _____ is **encouraged to resist** the **temptation to vocalize displeasure to** the **entire class** when things don't turn out as expected. (**N**)

- _____ has made **limited progress in areas** of **organizational skills**, **homework completion**, **social skills**, and **interpersonal relationships**. (**N**)

- _____ is **learning how to interact** in a **positive manner** with his/her peers and teachers. _____ **requires consistent reminders regarding** what is, and what is not, **appropriate interaction**. (**N**)

- **Interrupting** the **lesson** or **other speakers** takes away from the flow of classroom activities. _____ **needs to give others** a **chance to finish speaking** before **interrupting** with his/her own opinion. (**N**)

- _____ is **encouraged to listen** and **consider ideas** of **others without interrupting** and **being negative. Frequent vocal complaints** and **negative comments** continue to **undermine** our classroom learning environment. (**N**)

- _____ continued to **struggle** in the final term in the area of **social interaction** with others. _____ is **reluctant to accept responsibility for unsuccessful conversations** with others and **often engages** in **inappropriate "name-calling."** _____ is **encouraged to seek positive relationships** with others and **avoid friendships** with students **who have a negative effect on** his/her **behavior**. (**N**)

- _____ is **encouraged to resist** the **temptation to vocalize displeasure** to the entire class **when things don't turn out as expected**. (**N,N**)

- _____ often **speaks out of impulse**, with a **limited sense of when to speak** and **for how long. Frequent distractibility** and lack of focus (*are a **major concern**/ have often **hindered** successful **communication** with teachers and peers*). (**N,N**)

- _____ is experiencing **difficulty behaving** in an **appropriate** manner during class time, and **controlling** his/her **emotional outbursts**. Through teacher **support** and **guidance**, as well as **social skills strategies**, it is hoped that _____ will soon experience improvement in this area. (**N,N**)

Math Problem Solving

General

- _____ (*rarely/ sometimes/ often/ usually/ always*) **solves problems accurately. (G)**

- **Solves problems** (*with teacher assistance/ with limited assistance/ independently*). **(G)**

- Uses **problem-solving steps** and **methods** (*with assistance/ some assistance/ independently and accurately*). **(G)**

- Applies **problem-solving steps** and **methods** (but) with (*considerable/ minor*) **mistakes** and/or **exclusion** of information. **(G)**

- Solves problems by (*adjusting/ modifying/ Cchanging/ altering*) taught **strategles** with (*rarely/ some/ almost/ always*) accirate results (solutions). **(G)**.

- **Problems** are **solved** by choosing the **most appropriate method,** and the results (*rarely/ sometimes/ usually/ always*) lead to accurate results (solutions). **(G)**

- Solves problems with (*limited/ appropriate*) strategies (but **incomplete reasoning** and **explanation**) and (*rarely/ frequently*) **accurate results** (solutions). **(G)**

- _____ (*with teacher assistance/ sometimes/ often/ accurately and consistently*) _____ **selects appropriate units**, **tools**, **strategies,** and **computational methods** and applies them to problem-solving activities related to the _____ unit. **(G)**

- _____ carries out the required **computation skills** and **solves problems involving whole numbers** (**fractions** and **decimals**) (*with little accuracy/ with some accuracy/ accurately*) and (*with teacher assistance/ with some teacher assistance/ independently/ with absolute accuracy and confidence*). **(G)**

Positive

- Problem solving is an **area of clear** (definite) **strength** for _____. **(P)**

- _____ **works with effort** when performing (doing) problem-solving activities (tasks). **(P)**

- **Some progress** was **observed**, and _____ is **to be commended** for his/her **willingness** and **enthusiasm** to **succeed**. **(P)**

- _____ **shows** an **ability to recall problem-solving strategies** and use them in mathematics and (also) **everyday life**. **(P)**

- _____ carries out the required **computation skills** and solves assigned **problems involving whole numbers (fractions** and **decimals)** with (good deal of/ much) **accuracy.** _____ **perseveres through challenging tasks** and (usually/always) **tries hard** to follow through with the recommended **problem-solving process** (and steps). **(P)**

- _____ is able to **choose** and perform **computation techniques** (steps/ operations/ methods) **(addition, subtraction, multiplication, division) appropriate to specific problems** and **determine whether** the obtained **results** make sense. **(p)**

- _____ **consistently chooses appropriate units, tools, strategies,** and **computational methods** in problem-solving activities. He/she **effectively plans** and **organizes mathematical information** to create a **stratey** for solving complex problems. **(P)**

- _____ **continues to work well** on **problem solving** by applying and using the learned **strategies** and **steps.** _____ **works patiently** and **effectively with** his/ her **peers** in group problem-solving situations. **Steady progress is being** made in this area. **(P)**

- With **some teacher assistance,** and use of **recommended problem-solving strategies,** _____ is able to solve **simple mathematics problems.** _____ continues to show **excellent motivation** and **commitment** to successful solving (completion) of math problems. **(P)**

- _____ performs the required **computation skills** and solves **problems involving whole numbers** and **decimals** with (good deal of/ much) **accuracy.** _____ **perseveres through challenging tasks** and (usually/ always) **tries hard** to follow through with the recommended **problem-solving process** (and steps). **(P)**

- _____ **accurately** and **regularly chooses appropriate units, tools, strategies,** and **computational methods** in problem-solving activities related to the _____ unit. _____ **competently** and **confidently organizes mathematical information** to **create a plan** and solve the given problems. **(P)**

- _____ **shows excellent motivation** and **commitment** to solving math problems. Effective problem solving involves the use of all **steps** of the **problem-solving method.** _____ is encouraged to **become familiar** with the variety of **strategies** and then apply them to solving mathematical (**word**) problems. **(P)**

- _____ has **worked hard** and **demonstrated some improvement** in this area. He/she is **learning** to **re-read problems** and **select appropriate strategies** for **solving mathematical problems.** This is an area that should be **reinforced** (over the summer months/ next term) in order to retain the skill level that has been acquired to date. **(P)**

- With given **strategies,** positive **encouragement,** and regular **practice,** _____ is **becoming** more **aware** of his/her **ability to solve problems** and **experience success.** _____ is quickly learning that problems are **not always as difficult** as they are initially perceived to be. He/she is **encouraged to** continue to **persevere** with assignments that are more challenging. **(P)**

- With (taught/ provided/ learned) strategies, positive encouragement, and regular practice, _____ is **becoming more aware of** his/her **ability to solve problems** and experience success. _____ is **quickly learning** that **problems** are **not always as difficult as** initially perceived. He/she is **encouraged to continue to persevere** with assignments that are more challenging. (**P**)

Positive/Negative

- **Problems** are **solved** with **appropriate strategies**, but **incomplete explanations**. (**P,N**)

- _____ **responds well** to **provided assistance, when working through strategies** to solve problems. There are times, **however**, when **related review work has not been completed** (at home) as assigned. _____ needs to spend more time following through (at home) with assigned review work. (**P,N**)

- _____ **continues to require** a lot of **assistance with understanding and applying problem-solving concepts** in mathematics. He/she has been **very responsive** to **offered support** (in this subject). (**N,P**)

- _____ performs the required **computation skills** and **solves problems involving** whole numbers, fractions, and decimals with **some accuracy** and **teacher assistance**. _____ **perseveres through challenging tasks** and **usually tries** hard to **follow through with** the recommended **problem-solving steps**. (**N,P**)

- _____ still **struggles with taking risks** in mathematics and consequently **tries to avoid new challenges**. Provided **strategies** and **positive encouragement** in this area have been taught and, as _____ practices and **attempts to do the** questions, he/she is likely to **be more aware of** personal **ability** to solve (word/ mathematical) problems. _____ is **encouraged** to **continue to persevere** with assignments that are challenging. (**N,P**)

Negative

- _____ has **difficulty following** the **math problem-solving steps** in order to solve problems with success. (**N**)

- _____ **makes** (puts forth) a **good effort when solving assigned questions**. He/she **is encouraged to persevere** and discuss his/her reasoning (with an adult). (**N**)

- Problem solving is an area in which _____ **continues to struggle**. This seems to be the **result of** his/her **struggle with** the **decoding** (reading/ comprehension) of **written words** (information). (**N**)

- **Reviewing** and **memorizing the multiplication table at home**, as part of a daily homework routine, **would help** with **computational skills** and **solving of math problems**. (**N**)

- _____ still **struggles** with **taking risks** in **mathematics** and consequently **tries to avoid new challenges**. _____ is encouraged to continue to **persevere with challenging math problems**. (**N**)

- _____ **has had difficulty grasping an understanding of some of the math concepts** introduced this term. This is an area where **improvement could take place** with **more initiative** and **review** of **newly learned material. (N)**

- _____ **continues to struggle** with the **application of strategies** taught in class to solve math problems. **Remedial assistance** and **additional review at home would help** in becoming familiar and comfortable with the problem-solving process. **(N)**

- _____ **has worked hard** and **demonstrated some improvement** in this area. He/she is **learning** to **re-read problems** and **select appropriate strategies to use** when solving mathematical problems. This is an **area that** will be **reinforced throughout** the **year** in order to retain the acquired skill level. **(N)**

- _____ continues to **struggle** with the **understanding** and **application** of **math concepts. However,** _____ has been **responsive to assistance** from the **classroom teacher** (and teacher **assistant**). _____ is **encouraged to continue to ask questions** and **seek remedial assistance** when and if experiencing difficulty with specific areas of mathematics. **(N)**

- _____ has **difficulty working through** mathematical **problems. Multistep problems** that require **memorizing of information** often cause **frustration** for _____ as he/she is **unable** to **recall** all the necessary and needed **details**. Use of information, **chunking,** and **highlighting strategy would help** _____ (more readily) **access** the **information** he/she needs to solve math problems with more success. **(N)**

Report Card and IEP Comments

Math Comments - Variety

General

- _____ is **able** to _____, **but** often **struggles** with _____ in our mathematics program. (**G**)

- _____ is experiencing (*a great deal of/ some/ no*) difficulty with (is able to grasp effectively) **abstract concepts** (ideas). (**G**)

- _____ uses **order of operations** (to solve mathematical problems) (*with difficulty/ with some difficulty/ independently/ independently and accurately*). (**G**)

- _____ has **successfully completed** (*few/ some/ most/ all*) of the **requirements** of (*the mathematics curriculum/ this mathematics strand*) this term. (**G**)

- _____ has a (*limited/ inconsistent/ good/ excellent/ impressive*) **understanding** of **concepts** related to _____, _____, and _____. (**G**)

- _____ describes the **relationship** between [*insert here* **units of measurement**] (*with notable errors/ with several negligible errors/ with a few minor errors/ with practically no errors*). (**G**)

- **Computation skills** required in solving problems that involve **whole numbers** and **decimals** are applied (*with considerable teacher assistance/ with limited assistance/ independently/ effortlessly*). (**G**)

- _____ uses **calculator** (*only with teacher assistance/ with some assistance/ independently/ effectively and successfully*) to perform simple operations using **whole numbers** and **decimals** [*or… add other information here*]. (**G**)

- _____ (*only with assistance/ with assistance/ with some teacher assistance/ independently/ with ease, creativity, and confidence/ effortlessly*) identifies, evaluates, creates, and solves (simple, more complex) **algebraic equations** (**expressions**). (**G**)

- _____ carries out **operations** with (***whole numbers/ fractions/ decimals/ integers***) (*with difficulty/ with some assistance/ independently/ independently and accurately/ impressively and confidently*). (**G**)

- _____ **compares** and **orders numbers** (whole numbers/ fractions/ decimals/ integers, etc.) (*only with intense teacher assistance/ with some teacher assistance/ independently/ independently and effectively [accurately]*). (**G**)

- _____ is able to solve **multistep mathematical problems**, using different (appropriate) **strategies** (*only with teacher assistance/ with some assistance/ independently/ independently and accurately*). (**G**)

- _____ (*rarely and with limited accuracy/inconsistently and with some accuracy/ usually and with frequent accuracy/ consistently and with a higher level of accuracy*) **recalls multiplication** and **division facts to** _____. (**G**)

- _____ (*only with teacher assistance/ with assistance/ with some assistance/ independently/ with ease, creativity and confidence/ effortlessly*) identifies, extends, and (*creates/ analyzes/ discusses*) **models/ tables** of (basic, simple, more complex) **patterns**. (**G**)

- _____ is able to carry out **basic operations** involving (***whole numbers/ decimals/ fractions/ integers/ percent/*** etc.) (*with much difficulty/ only with teacher assistance/ with some assistance/ independently/ independently, accurately, and confidently/ effortlessly*). (**G**)

- _____ (*only with teacher assistance/ with some teacher assistance/ independently/ independently and consistently/ consistently*) works with and **interprets probability data** located in **tables**, **tally charts**, **line graphs**, and **bar graphs** to **solve** (*required/ simple/ more complex*) mathematical **problems**. (**G**)

- _____ **estimates**, **measures**, **compares**, and **records** (the **volume** of objects [name objects, if needed]/ the **mass** of objects using **standard units**/ **mass** and **capacity**/ the **perimeter** and **area** of [**rectangles**, **square**, **parallelograms**, **triangles**, etc.]) (*only with teacher assistance/ with notable errors/ inconsistently with several minor errors/ frequently with few minor errors/ consistently and accurately/ with accuracy, confidence, and ease/ effortlessly*). (**G**)

- _____ uses and applies learned **knowledge** of **probability** (*with difficulty/ with some difficulty/ accurately and quickly/ effortlessly*) to solve (*simple/ more complex*) problems. _____ **records** the **results** of **probability experiments** (*with major errors/ with several minor errors/ with **limited** errors*). **Probability data** is **interpreted** and **understood** (*with assistance/ with some assistance/ independently/ independently and consistently/ consistently/ effortlessly* and flawlessly). (**G**)

- _____ shows (demonstrates) an understanding of (identifies) (***points, lines, rays, angles/*** and ***translations, reflections,*** and ***rotations/ parallel*** and ***perpendicular lines/ estimating, drawing,*** and ***measuring angles/*** naming and identifying ***attributes*** of main [**2D** and **3D**] ***geometric shapes/ constructing*** [simple/ more complex] ***geometric models/ solving geometric problems/*** [or add other information here]) (*only with teacher assistance/ with some teacher assistance/ independently/ independently and accurately*). (**G**)

- _____ (*only with teacher assistance/ with some difficulty/ independently/ consistently*) **selects** relevant **units**, **tools**, **strategies**, and **computational methods** in **problem-solving** activities. He/she (*with difficulty/ with some difficulty/ independently/ independently and effectively*) **organizes** math-related **number** and **word information** to **create** a **plan** and **solve complex problems**. _____ is encouraged to **record solutions** to problems in an **organized** way, **showing all** important **work** and details. (**G**)

Positive

- **Problem solving** is an **area of** clear (definite) **strength**. (**P**)

- **Impressive**-looking **notebook**! Thanks for **setting** an **example** for others! (**P**)

- **Excellent growth** in area of naming the **place and value** of numbers has been noted. (**P**)

- **Reviewing multiplication** (*table*) **facts** at home, as part of a daily homework routine, **would help** with **computational skills**. (**P**)

- **Some progress** was **observed**, and _____ is **to be commended** for his/her **willingness** and **enthusiasm to succeed**. (**P**)

- **Further practice** of **multiplication facts** and **basic computational skills** is necessary in order to improve achievement in mathematics (this subject). (**P**)

- _____ **perseveres** through **challenging tasks** and usually (*always*) **tries hard** to follow through with the recommended **problem-solving process**. (**P**)

- _____'s **confidence with basic numeracy skills** continues to **increase** with ongoing classroom practice. **When unsure** of **instructions**, and **when additional clarification** is **needed**, _____ is encouraged to seek teacher **assistance**. (**P**)

- _____ **participates during math classes** by **offering answers** and **suggestions**. He/she **often attempts** to use **appropriate terminology** when providing input. _____ also **asks questions** to **clarify information**. **Rehearsal of the multiplication table** at home, one section at a time, **would help improve basic numeracy skills**. (**P**)

- _____ **is encouraged to work** on **memorizing** the **multiplication table** during the [*summer break/ Christmas holidays/ when no other homework is required*]. Through regular practice _____ is **learning** the **basic computational skills**. _____ is to be **commended for** his/her **willingness** and **confidence to participate** in class (our) math activities. (**P**)

- _____'s **confidence with basic numeracy skills has increased** with ongoing classroom practice. **When unsure** of the **instructions** _____ has learned to **ask questions** for **clarification** and **willingly accepts assistance** that is offered. **Practicing number facts** during the (*summer months/ holidays/ school break*) **would be beneficial** in **reinforcing** the math **skills** acquired to date. (**P**)

Positive/Negative

- _____ **continues to improve** in this area, **but** at a **slower pace**. **Verbal interruptions** and **negativity** by _____ are hindering learning. (**P,N**)

- Based on in-class observations since the beginning of this school year (term), _____ has **come** a **long way** in **learning** to **work independently** (and **developing**) and **maintaining more effective learning habits** (on his/her own). (**P,N**)

Negative

- Understanding more **complex topics** continues to be a **challenge**. (**N**)

- _____ has difficulty with the knowledge of basic **number facts**. (**N**)

- **Test results** indicate that _____ is an area of **difficulty**. (**N**)

- _____ is reminded to **work carefully** (slowly) to avoid **careless errors**. (**N**)

- **Basic computational skills** remain (unchanged) at a level similar to that of last year (term). (**N**)

- _____ continues to do all of his/her **homework** and **fully participate** in the math class. (**N**)

- **Higher degree** of **concentration** and **commitment** to tasks would produce improved results. (**N**)

- More effective **studying** for **tests** is **needed** to ensure future academic success in mathematics. (**N**)

- Greater effort and care are needed when **making notes** or **copying information** from the **blackboard**. (**N**)

- **Rehearsal** of the **multiplication table facts** at home, one section at a time, **would help improve basic numeracy skills**. (**N**)

- _____ **participates eagerly** in **discussions, but** often **needs reminders to settle down** and **focus** on the relevant topic. (**N**)

- Additional **re-teaching** of math **computational skills** needs to take place in order to assist _____ with future growth in mathematics. (**N**)

- **Rehearsal** of the **facts** that are **not yet committed to memory** is something that _____ can continue to do at home. (**N**)

- _____'s **comfort level** with math **problem solving** should improve with increased amount of **practice** and exposure at home. (**N**)

- **Problem solving** is an area in which it is **difficult** for _____ to experience growth, and this is mainly due to his/her **weak reading skills**. (**N**)

- _____ **rushes through** his/her **work** and often **ignores** the important **details**, which usually leads to **inaccurate** results and **lower marks**.(**N**)

- _____ has **difficulty remembering** the **steps** necessary for successful and accurate completion of the **whole number** and **decimal computational operations**. (**N**)

- _____ continues to have **difficulty understanding** some of the more **abstract concepts** and needs to be taught using the **"hands-on"** and **manipulatives** type of strategies. (**N**)

- **Rehearsal of the multiplication table** at home, one section at a time, would help improve basic numeracy skills. Likewise, it is **important** that _____ **study** for his/her **tests** and **complete all assigned homework on time**. (**N**)

Report Card and IEP Comments

- _____'s **study notes** are often **incomplete**, and math **workbooks** need greater **organization**. **Math materials** are frequently **neglected** and **not brought to class**, which makes it difficult for _____ to learn and participate in the math program. (**N**)

- **To improve** academic **achievement** in **mathematics**, _____ **needs to ensure that all homework assignments** are **completed** (and) **on time**. _____ also needs to **study for tests** and **ask questions** if and when math **concepts** are not understood. (**N**)

- _____ **is working on memorizing the multiplication table** in class. Our goal is to memorize the multiplication facts (to ten) (before the end of the year/term). Through regular practice, _____ **is learning the basic computational skills**. **Rehearsal of** the **multiplication table at home**, one section at a time, **would help** develop basic numeracy skills. (**N**)

Next Steps

- _____ is encouraged to **record solutions to problems** in an **organized way**, **showing all** important work and **details**. (**NS**)

Science

General

- _____ shows an **understanding** of (only a *few/ some/ most/ all*) of the **basic/taught concepts**. (**G**)

- _____'s science **notes** are (*rarely/ sometimes/ usually/ always*) **neat** and **well organized**. (**G**)

- _____regularly **volunteers "additional" information** in response to specific science questions. (**G**)

- _____ **understands** (*few/ some/ most/ all*) of the **concepts** taught in _____ class. (**G**)

- _____ has **worked diligently** on (*few/ some/ most/ all*) aspects of the science curriculum this term. (**G**)

- Written **test results** indicate a (*poor/ good/ very good/ excellent/ thorough/ effective*) **understanding** of concepts taught. (**G**)

- Even in science class, _____ continues to exhibit **good working skills**, **great attitude**, and a **strong desire to learn**. (**G**)

- _____ shows **understanding of** (*few/ some/ most/ all*) of the **concepts** related to the topic of _____. (**G**)

- _____ (*rarely/ sometimes/ most of the time/ consistently*) uses appropriate **scientific terminology** when reporting **observations**. (**G**)

- _____ (*rarely/ sometimes/ usually/ consistently*) **demonstrates understanding** that _____. (**G**)

- _____ shows **understanding** (grasp) of (*only a few/ more than half/ most/ all*) of the required **curriculum** taught within the _____ unit. (**G**)

- _____ shows (*little/ some/ good/ excellent/ thorough/ admirable/ surprisingly strong*) **awareness** and **understanding** of the **safety procedures**. (**G**)

- The expected (***knowledge/ expertise/ comprehension***) is (*rarely/ sometimes/ usually*) **communicated** with clarity during tests and other forms of evaluation. (**G**)

- (*Very little/ Little/ Moderate/ Satisfactory/ Excellent/ Admirable/ Better than Expected*) **progress** in unit on _____ has been observed. (**G**)

- _____ shows **understanding** of (*few/ some/ most/ all*) of the **basic** (main/ important) **concepts** taught in this term's _____ unit. (**G**)

Report Card and IEP Comments

- _____ (*rarely/ sometimes/ usually/ always/ consistently*) **communicates** with clarity/ confidence what he/she has learned in the science class this term. (**G**)

- _____ **gives explanations** showing (*limited/ partial/ nearly complete/ complete*) **understanding** (comprehension) of what has been taught during this term. (**G**)

- _____ **uses materials** and **equipment** (*only with teacher assistance and close supervision/ with some teacher assistance/ safely and independently/ effectively*). (**G**)

- _____ is **able to identify** (*explain*) (*with teacher assistance/ with some teacher assistance/ independently*) in our _____ unit this term. (**G**)

- _____'s **predictions**, **observations**, and **conclusions,** as they relate to our science **experiments**, show (*a little/ some/ very good/ excellent/ thorough/ masterful*) **understanding** of the subject. (**G**)

- _____ shows **understanding** of (*few/ some /most/ all or almost all*) of the **concepts** (ideas/ curriculum) taught this term, (*rarely/ sometimes/ usually*) providing complete (nearly complete) and thorough **explanations**. (**G**)

- _____ uses the **microscope** to accurately **locate**, **observe,** and **draw slide specimens** (*with considerable teacher assistance/ with some teacher assistance/ with only occasional teacher assistance/ without assistance and independently*). (**G**)

- _____ **plans** clear and **complete procedures** for conducting a **fair test**, while identifying and **controlling** listed **variables** (*with teacher assistance/ with some teacher assistance/ with little teacher assistance/ independently/ independently and accurately*). (**G**)

- **Predictions, observations,** and **conclusions,** as they relate to our science **experiments**, (*often required assistance and specific teacher guidance/ were lacking in detail and accuracy/ were written in much detail/ were done well and in detail/ were written well and as instructed*). (**G**)

- **Notes** and **written comments** in science (*are not recorded as instructed and the writing is often disorganized and difficult to read/ tend to be very short and often lacking in content/ need to be better organized and recorded as instructed in order to make studying for tests easier/ are neat, well organized, and written very effectively*). (**G**)

- _____ **applies** (*few/ some/ most*) of the **required skills** needed to demonstrate an **understanding** of _____. He/she is **able** to _____ (*with considerable assistance/ with some assistance/ with only occasional assistance/ without assistance*). _____ has **shown** the **required knowledge** (*only with teacher assistance/ with some assistance/ always with clarity and detail*). (**G**)

Positive

- _____ has demonstrated a **high degree of interest** in science class this term. (**P**)

- _____ **participates positively** and **with enthusiasm** in all of our science **activities**. (**P**)

- _____ always **volunteers** to help conduct (our) scientific **experiments** and **demonstrations**. (**P**)

- _____ (often) wants to be the **first** person to **verbalize predictions** and make statements regarding the performed/completed **experiments**. (**P**)

Negative

- Many of the concepts taught are (too) **difficult** for _____ **to understand**. (**N**)

- _____ continues to **require assistance with** the **writing portion** of our science program. (**N**)

- **Expressing answers** related to science and **communicating** explanations in **written form** are **difficult** for _____. (**N**)

- Some of the material taught in science class is **difficult** for _____ **to understand** without additional, or after-school, assistance. (**N**)

- **Writing sentences** that accurately express scientific **concepts**, **terms**, **ideas**, and **information** is a **challenge** for _____. (**N**)

- _____ is **unable to participate** in the **written part** of our science program due to his/her **difficulty with** the **written language**. (**N**)

Independent Thinking and Risk Taking

Positive

- _____ follows routines and **instructions independently**. He/she **sometimes solves problems** independently. (**P**)

- **Some progress** was **observed**, and _____ is **to be commended** for his/her **willingness** and **enthusiasm to succeed**. (**P**)

- _____ is an **independent learner** who is **diligent** in pursuing and **researching** information in **personal areas of interest**. (**P**)

- _____ **always completes** his/her **work independently**. _____ **welcomes new tasks** and **seeks new opportunities** for learning. (**P**)

- _____ **shows motivation**, **initiative**, and **self-direction**. _____ is **encouraged** to **analyze** and **accurately assess** the **value** and **meaning** of **information**. (**P**)

- _____ is always **striving to learn** as much as possible on a wide variety of topics and areas of interest. _____ **does not hesitate to share** learned information to his/her classmates during **oral presentations**. (**P**)

Positive/Negative

- Based on classroom observations, _____ has **come a long way** in **learning to work independently** and **develop more effective learning habits**. Adequate and regular **completion** of **homework remains** an **area that needs to improve**. (**P,N**)

- _____ **has made** a **conscious effort** this term **to improve** his/her **writing skills**. He/she is **often observed writing lengthy paragraphs** and **editing** his/her **completed** work. _____ is **encouraged to increase** his/her **repertoire** of **writing topics** by **taking a risk** and **exploring subjects** that may be **new** and **unfamiliar**. (**P,N**)

Memory Coping Strategies

General/Positive

- **Some progress was observed**, and _____ is **to be commended** for his/her **willingness** and **enthusiasm to succeed**. **(G,P)**

Positive/Negative

- **Higher degree of concentration** and **focus** in class **would help** _____ remember more of the taught curriculum. **Repetition of information, improved organizational skills,** and **colorful visual presentation** of **text** and **graphics** on the blackboard **continue to help** _____ **remember** important information. **(P,N)**

- **Use of electronic** and **computer spell checkers** is **helping** _____ **spell words correctly** without spending a great deal of time looking for strategies that work. It is at times **necessary to remind** _____ of the **importance of being focused** and carefully **listening** to **teacher instructions**. _____ is **learning to ask** for **instructions** to be **repeated**, as a coping strategy for auditory memory. **(P,N)**

- **Change in seating plan** has helped _____ **concentrate** more effectively on given tasks. With teacher assistance, _____ is learning to use his/her school **organizer** to help him/her record **important events, reminders,** tests, and **homework** assignments that need to be completed. **Repetition** and **colorful visual presentation** of **text** and **graphics** on the **blackboard** are **helping** _____ remember important information. **(P,N)**

Self-Advocacy

Positive

- _____ has **learned to take pride in** his/her **unique strengths**. (**P**)

- _____ is **learning to evaluate** and **adjust to new** and **unexpected situations by not overreacting** and by **seeking assistance** and **clarification**. (**P**)

- _____ is **becoming more aware** of **personal strengths** and **needs**, and **using them** to **participate successfully** in new classroom **activities** and learning situations. (**P**)

- _____ has **learned to take pride in** his/her **unique strengths**. _____ **played** an **important role** in a **drama presentation** for the entire school during a morning **assembly**. He/she is **more aware of how** he/she **learns** and has **used strategies to assist in coping** with **personal educational challenges**. _____ has **become more self-confident throughout** the **year** and **responds favorably to positive reinforcement, encouragement,** and an ongoing **friendly, nurturing** classroom **environment**. (**P**)

Positive/Negative

- _____ **is learning to evaluate** and **adjust to new, unexpected situations by not** overreacting and **by seeking assistance** and **clarification**. It is clear that _____ is **becoming more aware** of **personal strengths** and **needs**, and **using them** to **successfully participate** in **classroom activities and new learning situations**. _____ **is encouraged** to **resist** the **temptation** to **vocalize displeasure** to the entire class **when things don't turn out as expected**. (**P,N**)

Negative

- **Guidance services** have been made available for _____ to use, and numerous classroom **activities** organized to **help build self-esteem** and **encourage** progress in learning. However, **inconsistency in attitude** and **lack of classroom behavior** necessary for further growth **continue to hinder progress**. (**N**)

Next Steps

- _____ is encouraged **to hand in all assignments** by the due date. (NS)

- A next step for _____ would be to **contribute more in group discussions**. **(NS)**

- _____ is encouraged **to maintain** good **effort** throughout the second term. **(NS)**

- _____ is encouraged to **participate in class discussions** and **group activities**. **(NS)**

- _____ is encouraged **to stay focused** and **keep the socializing** to a **minimum**. **(NS)**

- _____ is aware of the need for **seeking remedial assistance** on a regular basis. **(NS)**

- _____ is encouraged **to express opinions more** often during class discussions. **(NS)**

- _____ is encouraged **to complete** his/her **homework on time** and **with care**. **(NS)**

- _____ is encouraged **to complete tasks consistently, on time**, and **with care**. **(NS)**

- _____ is encouraged to **assess** his/her **own work and identify goals** to strive for. **(NS)**

- _____ is encouraged **to use school organizer** and **complete all homework tasks**. **(NS)**

- _____ is encouraged to seek **remedial help** when **concepts** are **unclear** or difficult. **(NS)**

- _____ is encouraged to **approach all subjects and problems** with a **positive attitude**. **(NS)**

- _____ is encouraged **to continue completing** his/her homework **on time** and **with care**. **(NS)**

- _____ is encouraged **to put forth greater effort** in order to **accomplish personal goals**. **(NS)**

- _____ is encouraged to show more attention to **care** and **detail in class work** and **assignments**. **(NS)**

- _____ is encouraged **to seek teacher assistance** when **concepts** are **unclear** or **difficult**. **(NS)**

- _____ is encouraged to **participate more frequently** in class and **group discussions**. **(NS)**

- _____ is encouraged to **work on organizational skills** and **utilize class time more effectively**. **(NS)**

- _____ is encouraged to **continue to accept small challenges** and to **develop** his/her **self-esteem**. **(NS)**

- _____ is **reminded to work toward** his/her **personal best** and to **refrain from excessive socializing**. **(NS)**

- _____ is encouraged **to maintain his/her positive, responsible attitude** throughout the final term. **(NS)**

- _____ is encouraged **to seek assistance prior to tests** in order to ensure that **concepts** are understood. **(NS)**

- _____ is **reminded to work toward** his/her **personal best** and to **refrain from socializing** during lessons. **(NS)**

- _____ is reminded **to put forth initiative toward** all **written work** in order to experience further success. **(NS)**

- To be successful, _____ is encouraged to **combine a positive** and **responsible attitude** with **diligent effort**. **(NS)**

- _____ is encouraged **to develop confidence in** his/her **ability to communicate ideas** in **class discussions**. **(NS)**

- _____ is encouraged **to** demonstrate **responsibility in attendance, punctuality,** and **task completion**. **(NS)**

- _____ is often able to work cooperatively in small **groups**, yet has had **some difficulty working independently**. **(NS)**

- _____ is encouraged to **participate more fully in class** and **group discussions, sharing** his/her **opinions and ideas**. **(NS)**

- _____ is encouraged **to put forth** a **consistent effort** in **completing assignments on time** and **with care**. **(NS)**

- _____ is encouraged **to work on improving** the **neatness of written work, consistently,** in all subjects, and **submit it on time**. **(NS)**

- _____ is encouraged to **participate** in class and **group activities** and **ask questions** to **clarify meaning** and **ensure understanding**. **(NS)**

- _____ is encouraged **to express/ verbalize** his/her **opinions more often during class discussions** so as to **further develop leadership abilities**. **(NS)**

- _____ is encouraged **to be considerate of** his/her classmates **by refraining from frequent outbursts** and **focusing instead on personal academic progress**. **(NS)**

- Throughout the next term, _____ is encouraged **to continue to build on** previous **achievements and to**, improve **communication skills** and **level of self-confidence**. **(NS)**

- _____ is to be **congratulated on** his/her **achievements** and encouraged to **continue in this more positive, responsible manner** throughout the (final) term. **(NS)**

- _____ demonstrates a **good ability to work in groups** and **independently**. He/she is encouraged to **express** his/her **opinions more often** during class discussions. **(NS)**

- To further **improve** in this area, _____ must make an effort to **develop a writing plan** (outline, diagram, story map, etc.) as one of the first steps of the **writing process**. **(NS)**

- Timely **completion of homework** and **regular, daily use of** the **school organizer must be in place** if _____ is to continue to experience success in academic subjects. **(NS)**

- _____ is encouraged **to concentrate on achieving personal goals** for the final term, including a **willingness to take risk** and **explore new** and **more challenging learning situations**. **(NS)**

Evaluation Not Possible

- (*Most/ Some/ Few*) of the assigned tasks have **not been completed** or submitted for marking. **Achievement** is **based on those tasks that were completed**.

- Accurate, meaningful, and thorough **assessment** has been **hindered** this term **by frequent absence** from school.

- An **extended vacation/ absence period** has made accurate assessment of progress very difficult at this time.

- Accurate and meaningful **assessment** of _____ is **not possible** this term **due to** _____'s **insufficient participation.**

- Accurate and meaningful **assessment** of **reading ability** is not possible this term **due to** _____ **insufficient participation** in the reading activities.

- Accurate and meaningful **assessment** of _____ is not possible this term **due to** _____ **insufficient participation** in _____ activities.

- **Vast majority of written assignments were not submitted** for marking; hence, accurate and meaningful **assessment** of _____'s writing ability is **not possible**. (**G**)

- Due to the fact that **no work has been completed** for this subject, accurate and meaningful **assessment** of ability is not possible at this time. Please see **IEP** for detail.

- _____ **has not completed or submitted required work** in _____, **despite generous class time** and **remedial opportunities**; hence, accurate and meaningful **assessment** of _____'s (writing) ability is not possible.

Evaluation Based Only on Completed Work

These comments can best be assigned to students who have neglected to hand in some, most, or all of their work for evaluation.

- (*Most/ Some/ Few*) of the **assigned tasks have not been completed** or **submitted for marking**.

- (*Most/ Some/ Few*) of the **assigned tasks have not been completed** or **submitted** for marking. **Achievement** is **based only on** those **tasks that were completed**.

- Achievement is **based only on** those **tasks that were completed**.

- **Some achievement** is **based only on** those **tasks that were completed**.

- **The mark for** _____ is **based only on work that was submitted** for evaluation.

- _____ **neglected to finish any** of the required **work** for the _____ unit, **in spite of daily reminders** and **opportunities to work in class**. **The mark for** _____ is **based only on work that was submitted** for evaluation.

- _____ was **not able to demonstrate** an **understanding** of the **materials covered** in class, as he/she **did not begin** or **complete** any (some/ most) class **assignments**. _____ **did not seek additional assistance** although this **option was offered** to him/her on a daily basis.

Part II

Substitute Teacher Instructions Kit

Dear Substitute Teacher:

_____

_____

_____

_____

_____

_____

_____

_____

_____

_____

_____

_____

_____

_____

_____

_____

_____

Classroom Teacher: _____

Substitute Teacher Instructions Kit

Substitute Teacher **Instructions**

Classroom **Teacher**: _____ Class: _____ Room: _____ Home Tel: _____

School: _____ Tel: _____ Fax: _____

Principal: _____

Vice Principal: _____

Secretary: _____

WHERE THINGS ARE:

Lesson Plans: _____

Keys: _____

Teacher's **Binder**: _____

Manuals/Curriculum Guides: _____

Long-Range Plans: _____

Class **List**, Seating **Plan**: _____

Attendance Folder: _____

Photocopy Machine: _____ Access Number: _____

School **Timetable**: _____

Teacher **Timetable**: _____

Class **Supplies**: _____

The "**Office**" button: _____

Custodian's Room: _____

Audio-Visual Equipment: _____

Staff **Restroom**: _____

Chalk, Pencils, Paper, etc. _____

For **additional help** please contact this **teacher**: _____ Room: _____

Reliable students who can further assist you: _____

Teacher's Lounge/ **Staff Room**: _____

School Timetable

	Time
School Entry	
National Anthem, Announcements	
Homeroom/ Home Form	
LUNCH	
After-Lunch School Entry	
Period 1	
Period 2	
Period 3	
Period 4	
Period 5	
Period 6	
Period 7	
Period 8	
School Dismissal	
Remedial help, Extracurricular activities	
Duty:	

Substitute Teacher Instructions Kit

School Timetable

	Time
LUNCH	
Duty:	

Daily

Class Entry: _____
_____
_____

Attendance: _____
_____

Classroom Rules: _____
_____
_____
_____
_____

Discipline Policy: _____
_____
_____
_____
_____

Rewards: _____
_____

Homework: _____
_____

Materials/Supplies: _____
_____
_____

LUNCH: _____
_____

Restrooms: _____
_____

Water Fountain: _____
_____

Illness: _____
_____

Dismissal: _____
_____

Additional Instructions

Emergency Procedures

Fire/FireDrill:

_____
_____
_____
_____
_____
_____

Severe Weather:

_____
_____
_____
_____
_____
_____

Intruders, Violence:

_____
_____
_____
_____
_____
_____

Other:

_____
_____
_____
_____

Substitute Teacher Instructions Kit

School Discipline Policy

1. _____

2. _____

3. _____

4. _____

5. _____

6. _____

7. _____

8. _____

9. _____

10. _____

THE SEATING Plan

Class: _____

Blackboard

The Seating Plan

Teacher: _____

Room: _____

Class: _____

BACK OF CLASS

FRONT

The Seating Plan

Room: _____

BACK

FRONT

Class: _____

BACK

FRONT

Class: _____

Substitute Teacher Instructions Kit

BACK

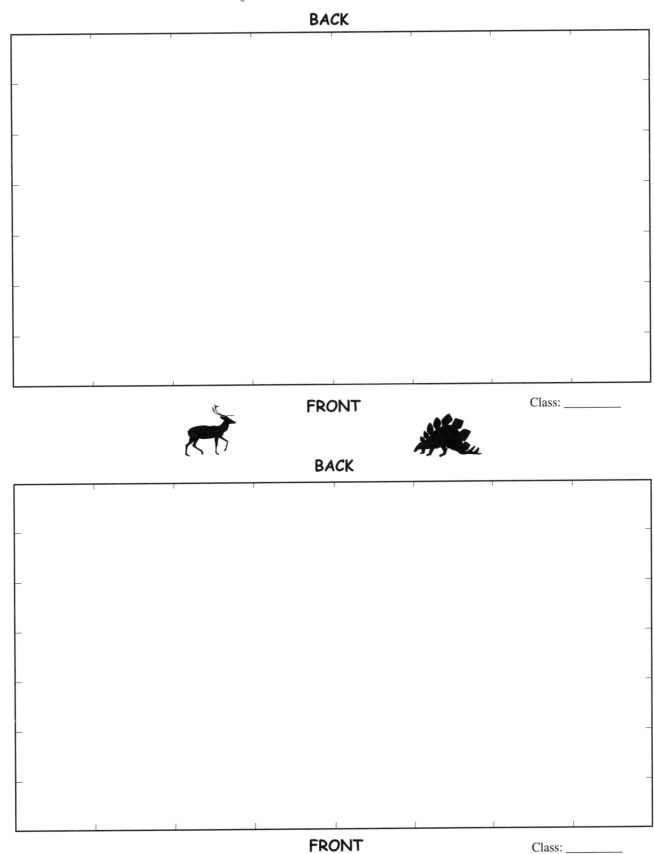

FRONT

Class: _____

BACK

FRONT

Class: _____

The Seating Plan

BACK

FRONT

Class: _____

BACK

FRONT

Class: _____

Student Name

Special Needs

	Health:
	Learning & Behavior:

	Health:
	Learning & Behavior:

	Health:
	Learning & Behavior:

	Health:
	Learning & Behavior:

	Health:
	Learning & Behavior:

Class List

Room: _____

Teacher: _____ Class: _____

Name	Date of Birth	Home ☎	Work ☎	Cell ☎	E-mail	Emergency Contact

Substitute Teacher Instructions Kit

Class: _____

NAME	FORM	☎		
1.				
2.				
3.				
4.				
5.				
6.				
7.				
8.				
9.				
10.				
11.				
12.				
13.				
14.				
15.				
16.				
17.				
18.				
19.				
20.				
21.				
22.				
23.				
24.				
25.				
26.				
27.				
28.				
29.				
30.				
31.				
32.				
33.				
34.				

CLASS LIST

Room _____

Teacher: _____ Class: _____

Name	☎	Locker Partner	Locker #	Lock Comb.	Lock Serial #

Substitute Teacher Instructions Kit

Class List

Room _____

Teacher: _____ Class: _____

Name	☎				

Class List

Room _____

Teacher: _____ Class: _____

Name		Date of Birth	Home ☎	Work ☎	Cell ☎	Emergency Contact

Substitute Teacher Instructions Kit

Class List

Class: _____
Room: _____
Teacher: _____

Special Education

Student Name	Integrated With
1.	
2.	
3.	
4.	
5.	
6.	
7.	
8.	
9.	
10.	
11.	
12.	
13.	
14.	
15.	
16.	

Functioning Levels

Date: _____

Class: _____

Student Name	Reading	Writing	Spelling	Oral Communication	Listening	Math Concepts	Math Problem Solving	Math Computation

Bus Students

Students arriving to school in a bus:

NAME				
1.				
2.				
3.				
4.				
5.				
6.				
7.				
8.				
9.				
10.				
11.				
12.				
13.				
14.				
15.				

Lesson Plan   Day: [ ]   Date: [   ]

✎ Reminder!

Per.	Class:	
Time:		

Per.	Class:	
Time:		

Per.	Class:	
Time:		

Per.	Class:	
Time:		

Per.	Class:	
Time:		

Per.	Class:	
Time:		

Per.	Class:	
Time:		

Per.	Class:	
Time:		

Photocopy:

💣 **Supervision Duties:**

Lesson Plan

Day: [ ]   **Date:** [ ]

✎ Reminder!

Photocopy:

💣 **Supervision Duties:**

Lesson Plan

Day: [ ]   **Date:** [ ]

✎ Reminder!

Per.	Class:	
	Time:	
Per.	Class:	
	Time:	
Per.	Class:	
	Time:	
Per.	Class:	
	Time:	

Lunch

Per.	Class:	
	Time:	
Per.	Class:	
	Time:	
Per.	Class:	
	Time:	

Photocopy:

💣 **Supervision Duties:**

LESSON PLAN

Week of:

	MONDAY	TUESDAY	WEDNESDAY

LUNCH

Photocopy:

Supervision Duties:

	THURSDAY	FRIDAY	Notes

LUNCH

Photocopy:

Supervision Duties:

LESSON PLAN

Week of: [   ]

	MONDAY	TUESDAY	WEDNESDAY
TIME:			
TIME:			
	LUNCH		
TIME:			
TIME:			

Photocopy:

Supervision Duties:

	THURSDAY	FRIDAY	Notes
TIME:			
TIME:			
	LUNCH		
TIME:			
TIME:			

Photocopy:

Supervision Duties:

Class: _____

HOMEWORK NOT DONE

Type:													
Student Name													

INCIDENT REPORT

Date: _____

Student Name: _____

Time of Incident: _____

Describe in detail what happened and why in your opinion it happened.

_____

_____

_____

_____

_____

_____

_____

_____

Did anyone else see what happened? _____

Was anyone hurt? _____

What strategies could have been used in order to avoid this incident?

_____

_____

_____

_____

Teacher's Comments: _____

_____

_____ Signature: _____

Parent's Comments: _____

_____

_____

Parent Signature: _____

Substitute Teacher Instructions Kit

Date: _____

Student Name: _____

Time of Incident: _____

Describe in detail what happened and why in your opinion it happened.

_____

_____

_____

_____

_____

_____

_____

_____

_____

_____

_____

_____

_____

Did anyone else see what happened? _____

Was anyone hurt? _____

What strategies could have been used in order to avoid this incident?

_____

_____

_____

_____

Teacher Notes: _____

_____

_____

_____

_____

Student Anecdotals

Name: _____

Period	Student Name	Anecdotal Notes

End of the Day
Feedback

Thank you for teaching my class in my absence. Please take a moment to write a brief note summarizing your experience and what was accomplished.

Teacher: _____

_____

_____

_____

_____

_____

_____

It would be helpful next time if: _____

_____

_____

Absent Students: _____

Helpful Students: _____

Disruptive Students: _____

Class Behavior:

Class: _____ ☐ courteous ☐ followed class rules ☐ needed reminders to remain on task

Class: _____ ☐ courteous ☐ followed class rules ☐ needed reminders to remain on task

Class: _____ ☐ courteous ☐ followed class rules ☐ needed reminders to remain on task

Class: _____ ☐ courteous ☐ followed class rules ☐ needed reminders to remain on task

Class: _____ ☐ courteous ☐ followed class rules ☐ needed reminders to remain on task

Class: _____ ☐ courteous ☐ followed class rules ☐ needed reminders to remain on task

Substitute Teacher's Name: _____ **Date:** _____

Thank you for teaching my class in my absence. Please take a moment to write a brief note summarizing your experience and what was accomplished.

Teacher: _____

Absent Students: _____

Helpful Students: _____

Disruptive Students: _____

Class **Behavior**:

Class: _____ ☐ courteous ☐ worked well ☐ needed reminders ☐ uncooperative (see note)

Class: _____ ☐ courteous ☐ worked well ☐ needed reminders ☐ uncooperative (see note)

Class: _____ ☐ courteous ☐ worked well ☐ needed reminders ☐ uncooperative (see note)

Class: _____ ☐ courteous ☐ worked well ☐ needed reminders ☐ uncooperative (see note)

Class: _____ ☐ courteous ☐ worked well ☐ needed reminders ☐ uncooperative (see note)

Class: _____ ☐ courteous ☐ worked well ☐ needed reminders ☐ uncooperative (see note)

Note: _____

_____

_____

_____

_____

_____

_____

It would be **helpful** next time if: _____

_____

Substitute Teacher's Name: _____ **Date:** _____

END OF THE DAY FEEDBACK

Thank you for teaching my class in my absence. Please take a moment to write a brief note summarizing your experience and what was accomplished.

Teacher: _____

_____

_____

_____

_____

_____

_____

_____

_____

It would be **helpful** next time if: _____

_____

_____

Class **behavior**:　☐ courteous　☐ followed class rules　☐ delightful!

☐ needed reminders　☐ uncooperative　☐ disrespectful (see note)

All **assigned work** was:　☐ completed　☐ not completed (see note)

Absent Students: _____

Helpful Students: _____

Disruptive Students: _____

Substitute Teacher: _____ **Date:** _____

END OF THE DAY FEEDBACK

Thank you for teaching my class in my absence. Please take a moment to write a brief note summarizing your experience and what was accomplished.

Teacher:_____

_____

Class **behavior**: ☐ courteous ☐ worked well ☐ delightful!

☐ needed reminders ☐ uncooperative (see note) ☐ disrespectful (see note)

All **assigned work** was: ☐ completed ☐ not completed (see note)

Absent Students: _____

Helpful Students: _____

Disruptive Students: _____

_____

_____

_____

_____

_____

_____

It would be **helpful** next time if: _____

_____

_____

Substitute Teacher: _____ **Date:**_____

Substitute Teacher Instructions Kit

END OF THE DAY FEEDBACK

Thank you for teaching my class in my absence. Please take a moment to write a brief note summarizing your experience and what was accomplished.

Teacher: _____

_____

_____

_____

_____

_____

_____

_____

_____

_____

_____

_____

_____

_____

_____

_____

_____

_____

_____

_____

_____

_____

Substitute Teacher: _____   **Date:**_____

Substitute Teacher Feedback

Thank you for teaching my class in my absence. Please take a moment to write a brief note summarizing your experience and what was accomplished.

Teacher: _____

Period	Comments

Absent Students: _____

Helpful Students: _____

Disruptive Students: _____

All **assigned work** was: ☐ Completed   ☐ Not Completed (see comments)

Substitute Teacher: _____

SUBSTITUTE TEACHER FEEDBACK

Date: _____

Thank you for teaching my class in my absence. Please take a moment to write a brief note summarizing your experience and what was accomplished.

Teacher: _____

Absent Students: _____

Helpful Students: _____

Disruptive Students: _____

All **assigned work** was: ☐ Completed   ☐ Not Completed (*see comments*)

Period	Comments

Substitute Teacher: _____

Date: _____

Thank you for teaching my class in my absence. Please take a moment to write a brief note summarizing your experience and what was accomplished.

Teacher: _____

Period	Comments

Substitute Teacher: _____

Substitute Teacher Instructions Kit

LIBRARY PASS

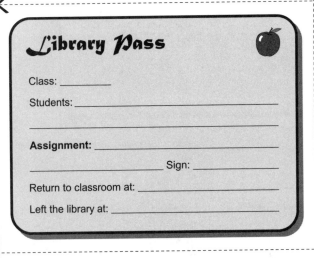

Library Pass

Class: _____

Students: _____
_____

Assignment: _____
_____ Sign: _____

Return to classroom at: _____

Left the library at: _____

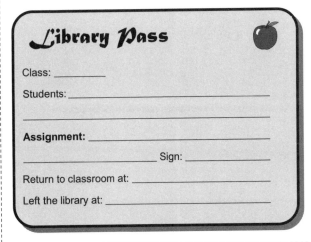

Library Pass

Class: _____

Students: _____
_____

Assignment: _____
_____ Sign: _____

Return to classroom at: _____

Left the library at: _____

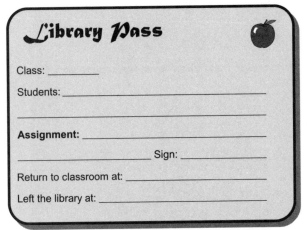

Library Pass

Class: _____

Students: _____
_____

Assignment: _____
_____ Sign: _____

Return to classroom at: _____

Left the library at: _____

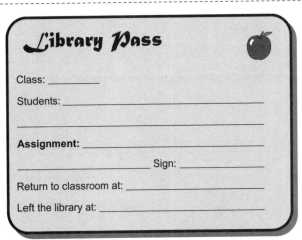

Library Pass

Class: _____

Students: _____
_____

Assignment: _____
_____ Sign: _____

Return to classroom at: _____

Left the library at: _____

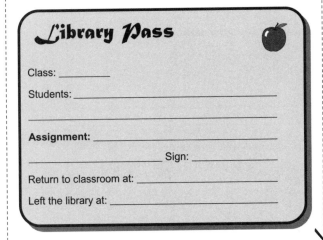

Library Pass

Class: _____

Students: _____
_____

Assignment: _____
_____ Sign: _____

Return to classroom at: _____

Left the library at: _____

Library Pass

Class: _____

Students: _____
_____

Assignment: _____
_____ Sign: _____

Return to classroom at: _____

Left the library at: _____

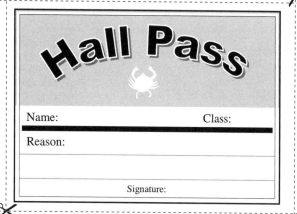

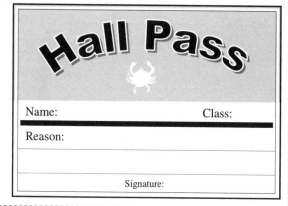

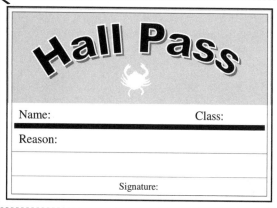

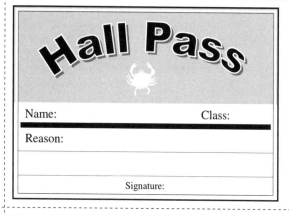

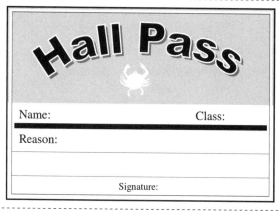

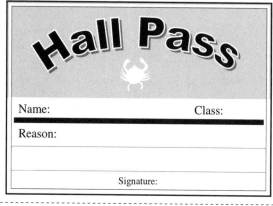

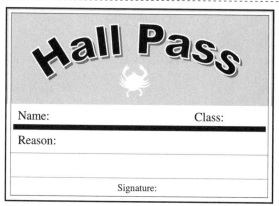

Reward students for outstanding achievement.

Student of the Day

_____ recognizes _____ Class: _____

For: _____

_____

Signed: _____ Dated: _____

Student of the Week

_____ recognizes _____ Class: _____

For: _____

_____

Signed: _____ Dated: _____

Thank You!

To: _____
_____
_____
_____

Teacher: _____
Date: _____

- ✂

THANK YOU!

To: _____
_____
_____
_____

Teacher: _____
Date: _____

- ✂

THANK YOU!

To: _____
_____
_____
_____

Teacher: _____
Date: _____

Substitute Teacher Instructions Kit

THANK YOU!

To: _____

_____

_____

Teacher: _____

Date: _____

✂- -

Thank You!

To: _____

_____

_____

Teacher: _____

Date: _____

✂- -

Thanks!

To: _____

_____

_____

Teacher: _____

Date: _____

Leaving the Room ?

Date: _____

Class: _____

STUDENT NAME	TIME OUT	REASON FOR LEAVING	TIME IN

Substitute Teacher Instructions Kit

Timesaving Substitute Tips

- **Arrive** to school early to ensure plenty of preparation time.

- Locate and read **teacher's notes** as soon as possible.

- Locate the classroom **key** and **organize** the supplies, handouts, and other equipment prior to class entry.

- If you need **assistance** seek it immediately.

- Follow the regular classroom **program** and **daily routines** as closely as possible.

- Prevent inappropriate student behavior by establishing yourself as an **authority figure** early. Speak and act decisively. Be firm but fair.

- Become **familiar** with the classroom **discipline policy** and **routines** and deal with undesirable incidents quickly and decisively. Indecision may lead to undesirable deterioration in behavior.

- Get the students involved in **meaningful activities** as soon as possible.

- Permit students to **exit** the classroom one person at a time. Have the students sign the "Leaving the Room?" sheet. This helps monitor student absence and promotes a structured class environment.

- At the end of the day leave a **note** for the classroom teacher summarizing what was accomplished and any areas of difficulty encountered by the students. Teachers appreciate being informed of what has occurred in their absence.

- Leave a **clean** and **tidy** classroom prior to departure.

- **Supervise** assigned detentions and **duties**.

- Offer to **assist** students with work after the regular school hours.

- Report accidents or serious problems to the principal.

- Inform the office of your **departure** and ask if you would be needed again.

- Go **home**, put up your feet, enjoy your family, watch a relaxing show, enjoy a snack!

Substitute Teacher Instructions Kit

Classroom Awards and Passes

Certificate of Appreciation

Awarded to:

For:

SIGNATURE

DATE

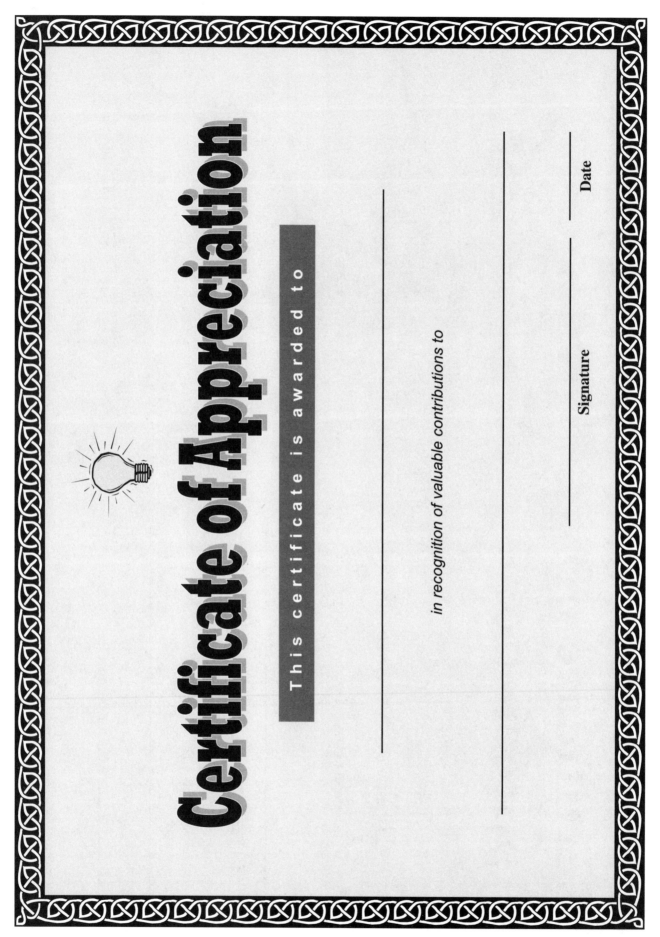

Certificate of Appreciation

This certificate is awarded to

in recognition of valuable contributions to

Signature

Date

Certificate of Appreciation

Presented to:

_____

Teacher Signature

_____

Date

CERTIFICATE OF APPRECIATION

This certificate is awarded to:

in recognition of valuable contributions to

Signature

Date

School

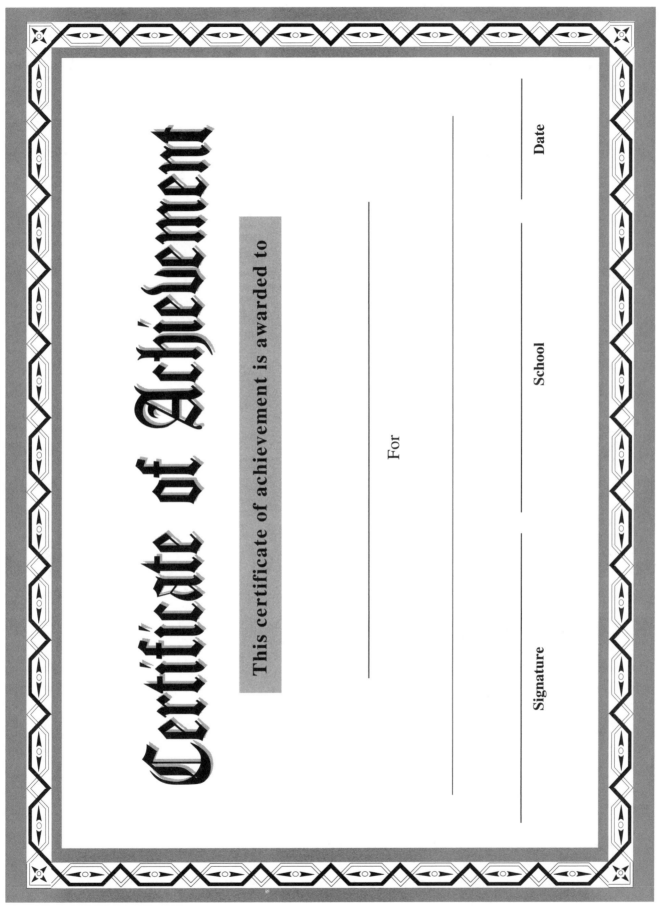

Certificate of Achievement

This certificate of achievement is awarded to

For

_____

School

_____

Signature

_____

Date

42ds

Certificate of Achievement

This certifies that

has successfully

Signature

Date

Certificate of Accomplishment

This certifies that

_____

has successfully completed

_____
Signature

_____
Date

Recognition Award Certificate

Presented to:

For: _____

_____
Signature

_____
Date

Special Achievement Award

Presented to:

For:

Signature

Date

Certificate of Merit

Awarded to:

For: _____

_____

_____

_____
Signature

_____
Date

Excellence Award

Awarded to:

For:

_____

_____ _____
Signature   Date

Outstanding Effort

Awarded to:

For: _____

Signature

Date

CERTIFICATE OF OUTSTANDING PERFORMANCE

This certificate is awarded to:

in recognition of:

Signature

Date

School

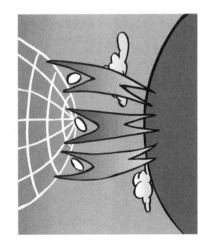

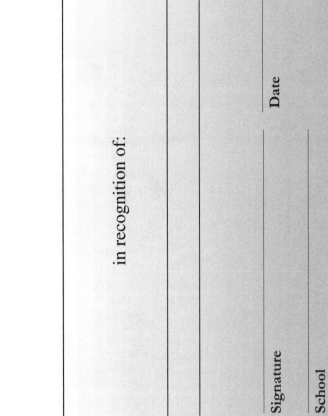

Perfect Attendance Award

Presented to:

_____

in recognition of perfect attendance!

_____
Date

_____
Signature

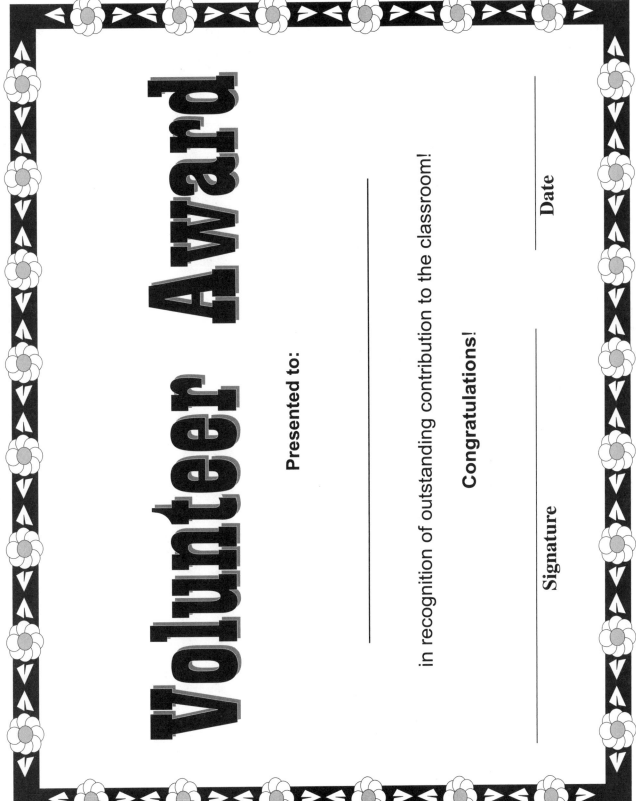

Volunteer Award

Presented to:

in recognition of outstanding contribution to the classroom!

Congratulations!

_____
Signature

_____
Date

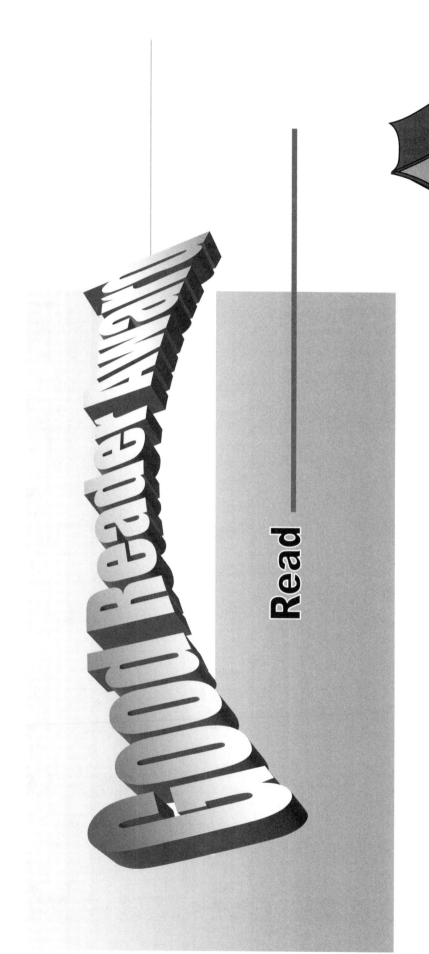

Good Reader Award

Read

Presented to:

Teacher Signature

Date

226

Good Conduct Award

For:

_____

Teacher Signature

_____

Date

Act of Kindness Award

Awarded to:

For:

_____

_____

_____

Signature

_____

Date

Class Participation Award

Presented to:

For: _____

Signature _____

Date _____

School _____

Star Student

For:

_____

Teacher Signature

_____
School

_____
Date

Student of the Day

Presented to:

_____

_____
Teacher Signature

_____
Date

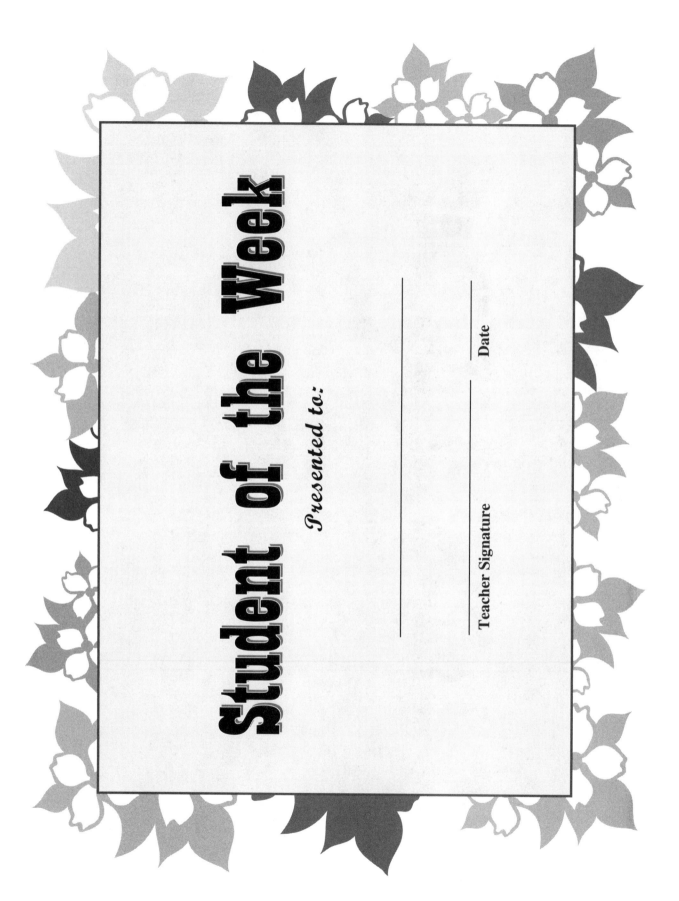

Student of the Week

Presented to:

_____

Teacher Signature

_____

Date

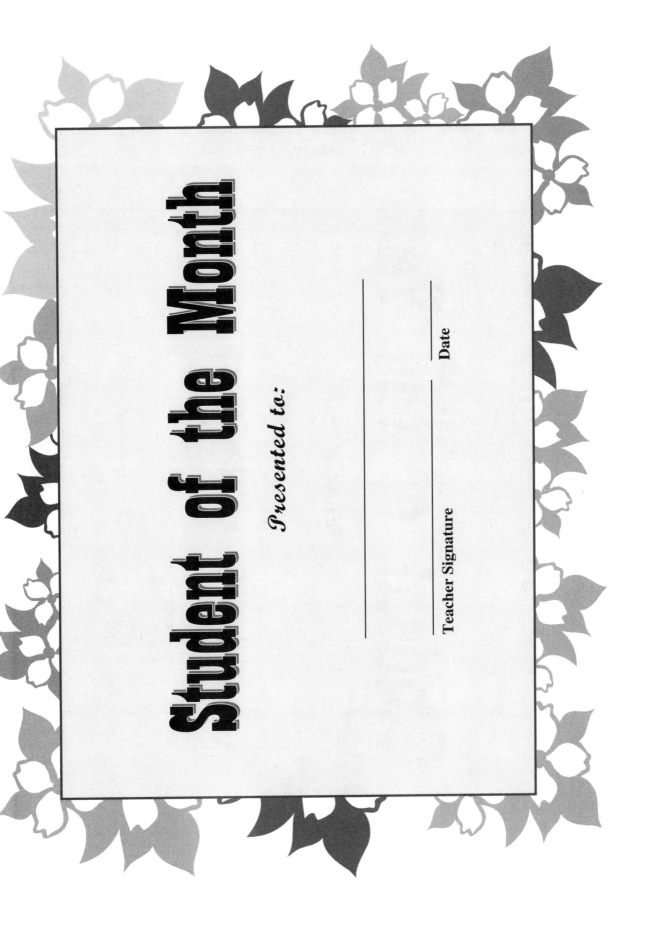

Student of the Month

Presented to:

_____

Teacher Signature

_____
Date

Student of the Year

Presented to:

_____

_____
Date

_____
Teacher Signature

Most Improved Student

This award is presented to:

_____

Teacher Signature

_____

Date

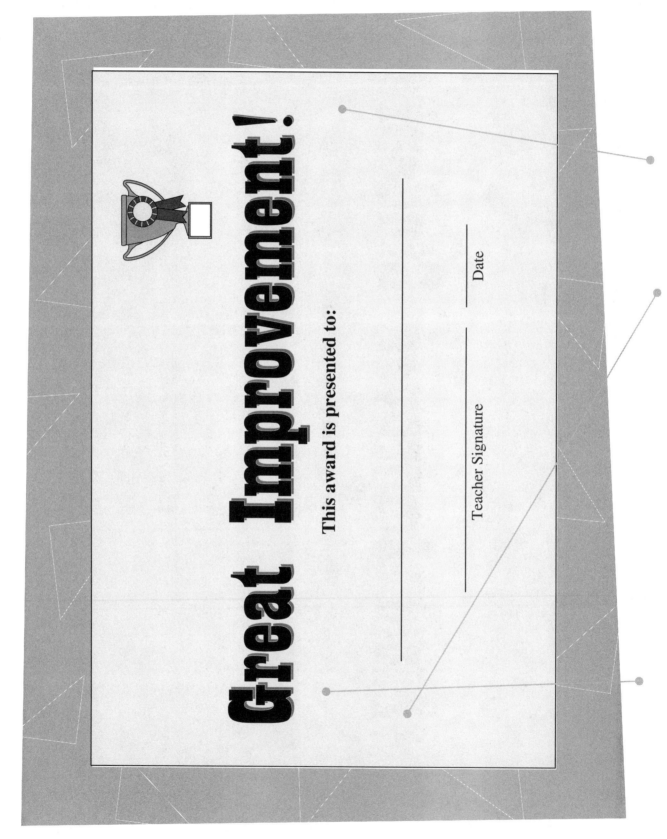

Great Improvement!

This award is presented to:

_____
Teacher Signature

_____
Date

Star Performance Award

Presented to:

For:

Signature

Date

School

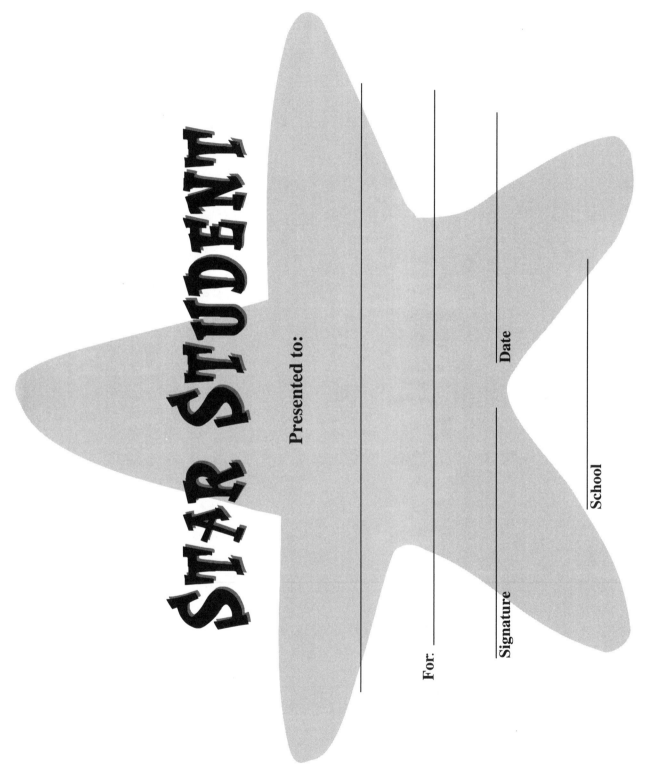

Star Student

Presented to:

For:

Signature

Date

School

Classroom Awards and Passes

You Are a Star!

Presented to:

For:

Signature

Date

School

You Are Number 1

Presented to:

_____

For: _____

Signature _____

Date _____

School _____

Great Ideas Award

Great Ideas

Presented to:

For:

Signature

Date

School

Classroom Helper Award

Awarded to:

For:

SIGNATURE

DATE

Good Helper Award

Awarded to:

For:

SIGNATURE

DATE

Congratulations!

For:

_____

Teacher Signature

_____
Date

_____
School

Outstanding Effort

Presented to

_____

In recognition of outstanding effort and great attitude toward learning.

Congratulations!

_____
Signature

_____
Date

Enthusiastic Participant Award

Awarded to:

_____

Signature

_____

Date

PAYS ATTENTION   LISTENS WELL TO OTHERS   HELPS OTHERS LISTEN WELL   GIVES OTHERS A CHANCE TO SPEAK

Attentive Listener Award

Awarded to:

_____

Signature

_____

Date

KNOWS WHEN TO SPEAK AND WHEN TO BE QUIET   RESPECTS OPINIONS OF OTHERS   RAISES HAND TO ASK A QUESTION

Classroom Awards and Passes

Having a Great Day Award

Awarded to:

Signature

Date

INCREDIBLE!

Awarded to:

Signature

Date

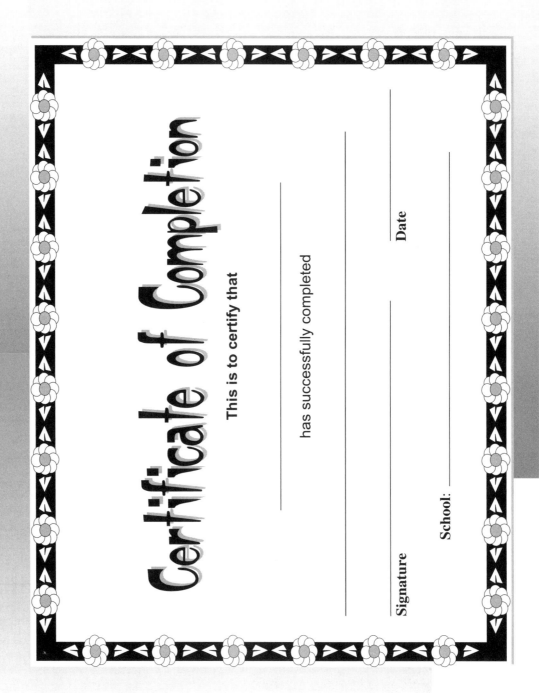

Certificate of Completion

This is to certify that

_____

has successfully completed

_____

Signature

School: _____

Date

Citizenship Award

Presented to:

In recognition of:

Signature

Date

Good Citizenship Award

Presented to:

In recognition of:

_____

_____
Date

_____
Signature

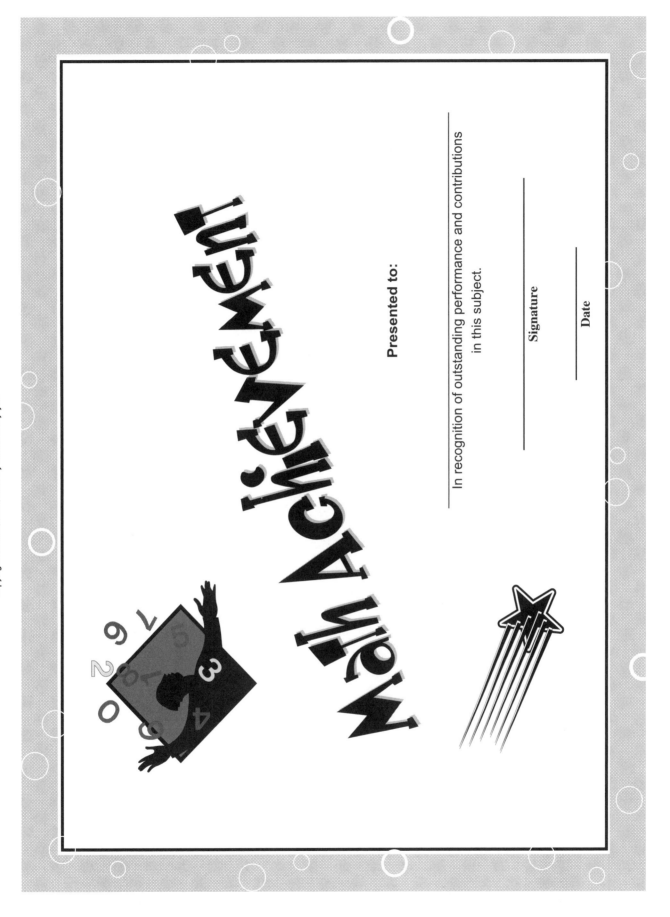

Math Achievement

Presented to:

In recognition of outstanding performance and contributions in this subject.

Signature

Date

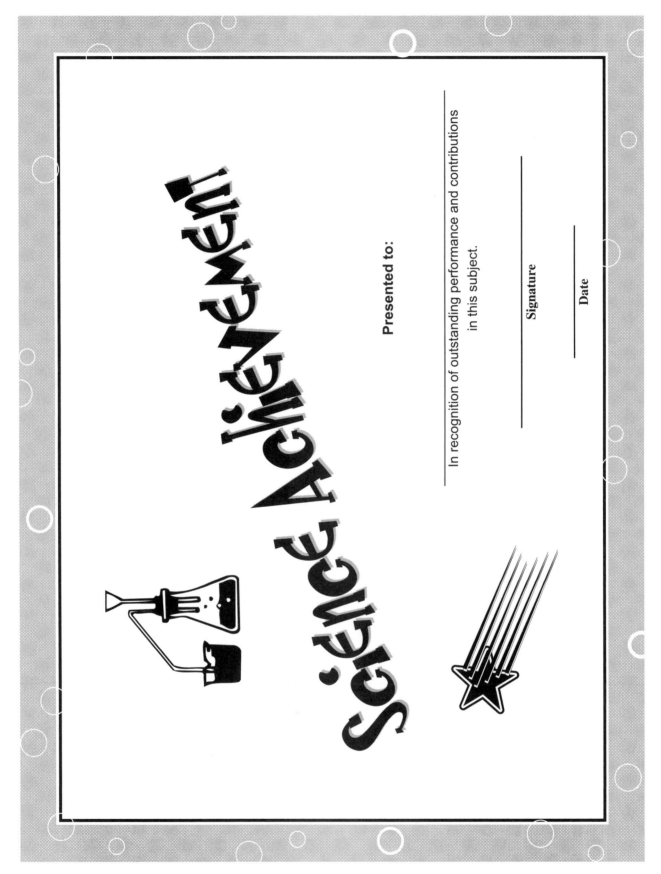

Science Achievement

Presented to:

In recognition of outstanding performance and contributions in this subject.

_____
Signature

_____
Date

Language Achievement

Presented to:

_____

In recognition of outstanding performance and contributions in this subject.

Signature _____

Date _____

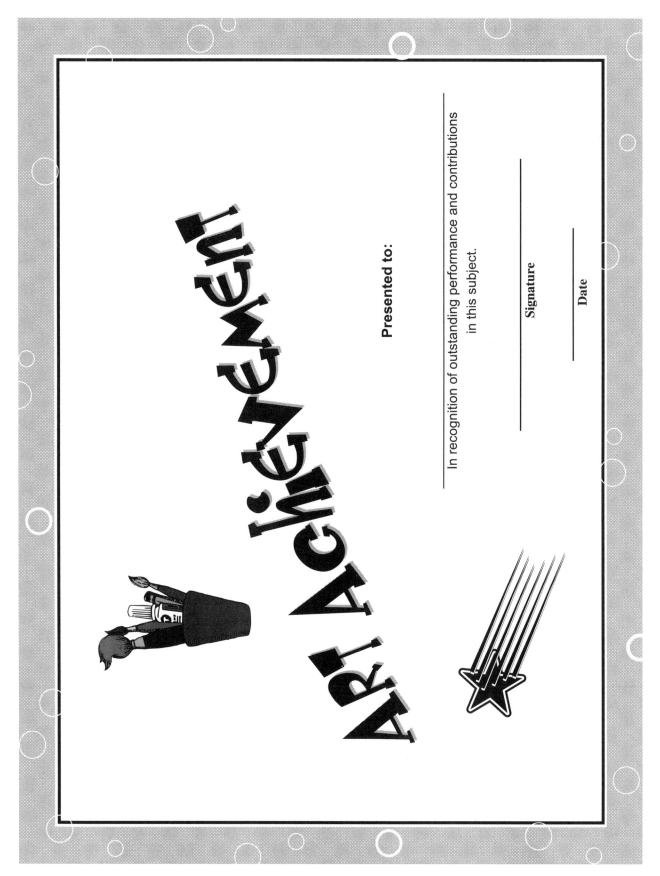

ART Achievement

Presented to:

_____

In recognition of outstanding performance and contributions in this subject.

_____
Signature

_____
Date

Sports Achievement

Presented to:

In recognition of outstanding performance and contributions in this subject.

_____
Signature

_____
Date

Music Achievement

Presented to:

In recognition of outstanding performance and contributions in this subject.

_____
Signature

_____
Date

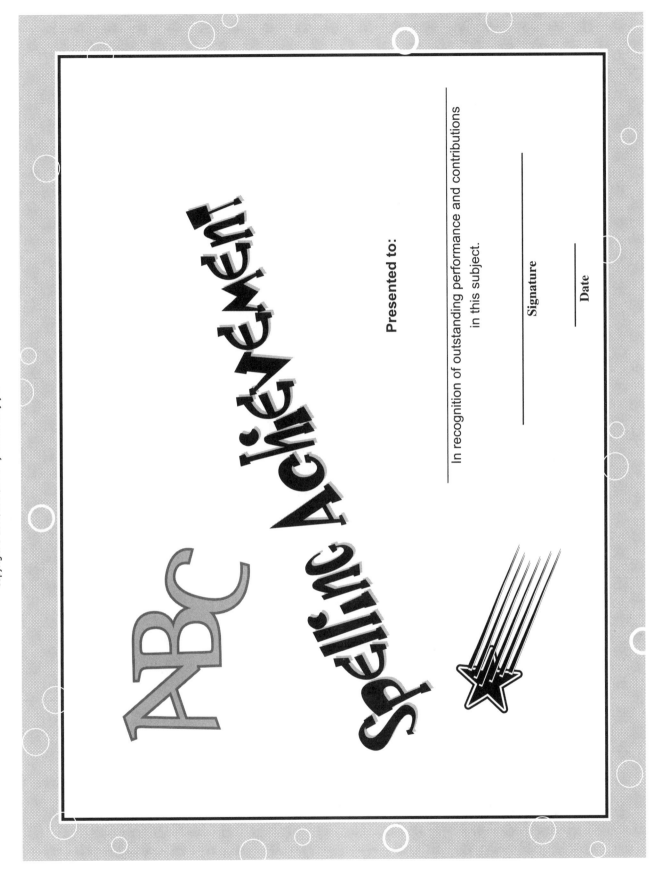

ABC

Spelling Achievement

Presented to:

In recognition of outstanding performance and contributions in this subject.

_____
Signature

_____
Date

Just Multiply I*#!

This is to certify that

_____

has successfully memorized the entire multiplication table!

Congratulations!

Signature _____

School : _____

Date _____

THANK YOU!

To: _____

_____

_____

_____

Teacher: _____

Date: _____

Thank You!

To: _____

_____

_____

_____

Teacher: _____

Date: _____

Thanks!

To: _____

_____

_____

_____

Teacher: _____

Date: _____

Thank You!

To: _____

_____

_____

_____

Teacher: _____

Date: _____

✂ -

THANK YOU!

To: _____

_____

_____

_____

Teacher: _____

Date: _____

✂ -

THANK YOU!

To: _____

_____

_____

_____

Teacher: _____

Date: _____

Thank You

For Your Help!

_____
Teacher

_____
Date

Thank You

For Your Help!

_____
Teacher

_____
Date

FOR PARTICIPATING!

_____

Teacher

_____

Date

FOR PARTICIPATING!

_____

Teacher

_____

Date

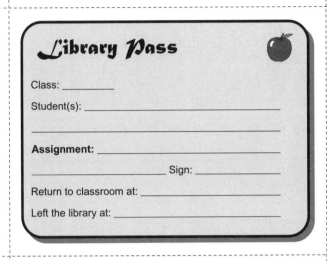

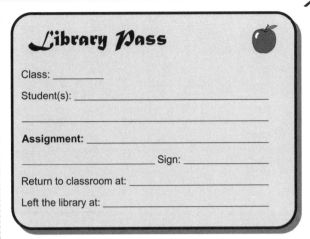

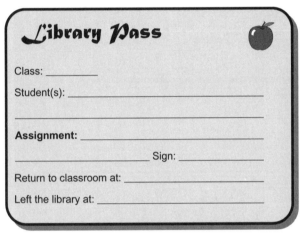

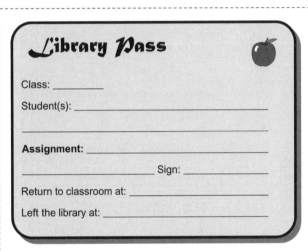

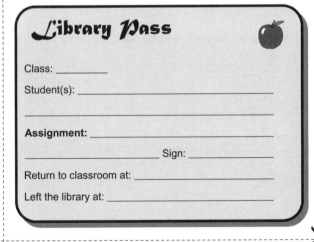

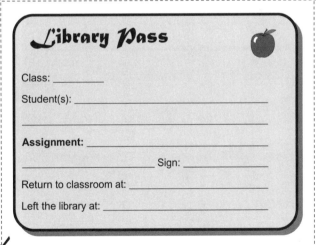

Classroom Awards and Passes

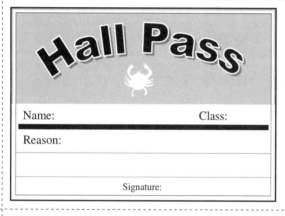

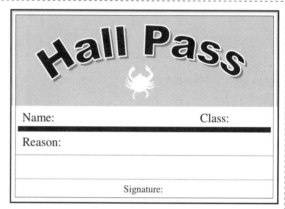

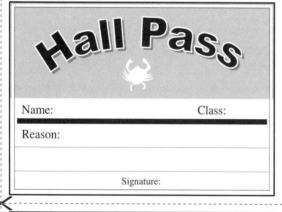

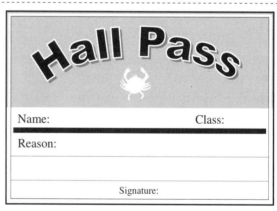

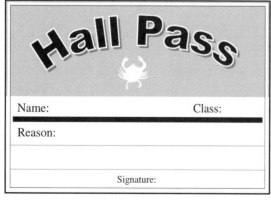

Classroom Awards and Passes

Name: _____ Class: _____

Is permitted to use the computer this period.

Signed: _____

Name: _____ Class: _____

Is permitted to use the computer this period.

Signed: _____

Name: _____ Class: _____

Is permitted to use the computer this period.

Signed: _____

Name: _____ Class: _____

Is permitted to use the computer this period.

Signed: _____

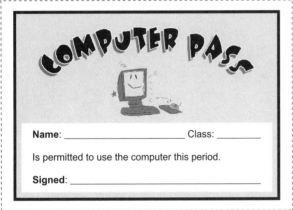

Name: _____ Class: _____

Is permitted to use the computer this period.

Signed: _____

Name: _____ Class: _____

Is permitted to use the computer this period.

Signed: _____

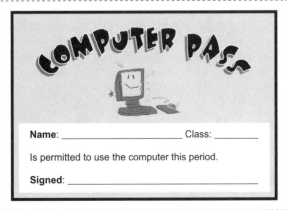

Name: _____ Class: _____

Is permitted to use the computer this period.

Signed: _____

Name: _____ Class: _____

Is permitted to use the computer this period.

Signed: _____

The holder of this pass is entitled to **one period** of uninterrupted use of classroom **computer**.

Signed: _____

The holder of this pass is entitled to **one period** of uninterrupted use of classroom **computer**.

Signed: _____

The holder of this pass is entitled to **one period** of uninterrupted use of classroom **computer**.

Signed: _____

The holder of this pass is entitled to **one period** of uninterrupted use of classroom **computer**.

Signed: _____

The holder of this pass is entitled to **one period** of uninterrupted use of classroom **computer**.

Signed: _____

The holder of this pass is entitled to **one period** of uninterrupted use of classroom **computer**.

Signed: _____

The holder of this pass is entitled to **one period** of uninterrupted use of classroom **computer**.

Signed: _____

The holder of this pass is entitled to **one period** of uninterrupted use of classroom **computer**.

Signed: _____

Bathroom Pass

Permission is granted to:

Name: _____ **Class:** _____
Signed: _____

Bathroom Pass

Permission is granted to:

Name: _____ **Class:** _____
Signed: _____

Bathroom Pass

Permission is granted to:

Name: _____ **Class:** _____
Signed: _____

Bathroom Pass

Permission is granted to:

Name: _____ **Class:** _____
Signed: _____

Bathroom Pass

Permission is granted to:

Name: _____ **Class:** _____
Signed: _____

Bathroom Pass

Permission is granted to:

Name: _____ **Class:** _____
Signed: _____

Bathroom Pass

Permission is granted to:

Name: _____ **Class:** _____
Signed: _____

Bathroom Pass

Permission is granted to:

Name: _____ **Class:** _____
Signed: _____

OFFICE PASS

Class: _____

Student Name: _____

_____

Reason: _____

_____ Sign: _____

Left the office at: _____

Returned to classroom at:_____

OFFICE PASS

Class: _____

Student Name: _____

_____

Reason: _____

_____ Sign: _____

Left the office at: _____

Returned to classroom at:_____

OFFICE PASS

Class: _____

Student Name: _____

_____

Reason: _____

_____ Sign: _____

Left the office at: _____

Returned to classroom at:_____

OFFICE PASS

Class: _____

Student Name: _____

_____

Reason: _____

_____ Sign: _____

Left the office at: _____

Returned to classroom at:_____

OFFICE PASS

Class: _____

Student Name: _____

_____

Reason: _____

_____ Sign: _____

Left the office at: _____

Returned to classroom at:_____

OFFICE PASS

Class: _____

Student Name: _____

_____

Reason: _____

_____ Sign: _____

Left the office at: _____

Returned to classroom at:_____

Game Pass

This pass entitles _____ to a game
session of _____ **minutes** in length.

Activity:_____

    Date Used: _____

Game Pass

This pass entitles _____ to a game
session of _____ **minutes** in length.

Activity:_____

    Date Used: _____

Game Pass

This pass entitles _____ to a game
session of _____ **minutes** in length.

Activity:_____

    Date Used: _____

Game Pass

This pass entitles _____ to a game
session of _____ **minutes** in length.

Activity:_____

    Date Used: _____

Game Pass

This pass entitles _____ to a game
session of _____ **minutes** in length.

Activity:_____

    Date Used: _____

Game Pass

This pass entitles _____ to a game
session of _____ **minutes** in length.

Activity:_____

    Date Used: _____

FREE TIME Pass

FREE TIME FREE TIME FREE TIME

This pass entitles_____

to _____ minutes of **FREE TIME**.

Date used: _____

Teacher Signature: _____

FREE TIME Pass

FREE TIME FREE TIME FREE TIME

This pass entitles_____

to _____ minutes of **FREE TIME**.

Date used: _____

Teacher Signature: _____

FREE TIME Pass

FREE TIME FREE TIME FREE TIME

This pass entitles_____

to _____ minutes of **FREE TIME**.

Date used: _____

Teacher Signature: _____

FREE TIME Pass

FREE TIME FREE TIME FREE TIME

This pass entitles_____

to _____ minutes of **FREE TIME**.

Date used: _____

Teacher Signature: _____

FREE TIME Pass

FREE TIME FREE TIME FREE TIME

This pass entitles_____

to _____ minutes of **FREE TIME**.

Date used: _____

Teacher Signature: _____

FREE TIME Pass

FREE TIME FREE TIME FREE TIME

This pass entitles_____

to _____ minutes of **FREE TIME**.

Date used: _____

Teacher Signature: _____

Classroom Awards and Passes

SPECIAL JOB ... SPECIAL JOB ...

This pass entitles_____

to perform a **special job**: _____

Job **Date**: _____

Teacher **Signature**: _____

SPECIAL JOB ... SPECIAL JOB ...

This pass entitles_____

to perform a **special job**: _____

Job **Date**: _____

Teacher **Signature**: _____

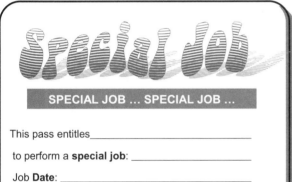

SPECIAL JOB ... SPECIAL JOB ...

This pass entitles_____

to perform a **special job**: _____

Job **Date**: _____

Teacher **Signature**: _____

SPECIAL JOB ... SPECIAL JOB ...

This pass entitles_____

to perform a **special job**: _____

Job **Date**: _____

Teacher **Signature**: _____

SPECIAL JOB ... SPECIAL JOB ...

This pass entitles_____

to perform a **special job**: _____

Job **Date**: _____

Teacher **Signature**: _____

SPECIAL JOB ... SPECIAL JOB ...

This pass entitles_____

to perform a **special job**: _____

Job **Date**: _____

Teacher **Signature**: _____

NO HOMEWORK!

NO HOMEWORK … NO HOMEWORK …

This pass entitles_____

to a **NIGHT WITH NO HOMEWORK.**

Date Used: _____

Teacher **Signature:** _____

NO HOMEWORK!

NO HOMEWORK … NO HOMEWORK …

This pass entitles_____

to a **NIGHT WITH NO HOMEWORK.**

Date Used: _____

Teacher **Signature:** _____

NO HOMEWORK!

NO HOMEWORK … NO HOMEWORK …

This pass entitles_____

to a **NIGHT WITH NO HOMEWORK.**

Date Used: _____

Teacher **Signature:** _____

NO HOMEWORK!

NO HOMEWORK … NO HOMEWORK …

This pass entitles_____

to a **NIGHT WITH NO HOMEWORK.**

Date Used: _____

Teacher **Signature:** _____

NO HOMEWORK!

NO HOMEWORK … NO HOMEWORK …

This pass entitles_____

to a **NIGHT WITH NO HOMEWORK.**

Date Used: _____

Teacher **Signature:** _____

NO HOMEWORK!

NO HOMEWORK … NO HOMEWORK …

This pass entitles_____

to a **NIGHT WITH NO HOMEWORK.**

Date Used: _____

Teacher **Signature:** _____